Choosing a Future
for U.S. Missions

CHOOSING A
FUTURE
FOR U.S. MISSIONS

Paul McKaughan
Dellana O'Brien
William O'Brien

800 West Chestnut Avenue, Monrovia, California 91016-3198 USA

Choosing a Future for U.S. Missions
Paul E. McKaughan, Dellanna W. O'Brien, William R. O'Brien

ISBN 1-887983-07-4

Published by MARC, a division of World Vision, 800 West Chestnut Avenue, Monrovia, California 91016-3198 U.S.A.

Printed in the United States of America. Cover design: Richard Sears.

Authors' Statement

We engaged in the Task Force: 21st Century Missions project as listeners, interpreters and commentators. We participated, not as critical outsiders, but as missioners who bring almost 100 years of mission service among the three of us. We are insiders. We have been part of the traditions and decisions that reflect late twentieth-century evangelical mission realities, and share the outcomes together. We share these insights humbly with our own Great Commission community in the hope that they will help all of us move obediently and courageously into the next century on a mission with our God to disciple the nations.

Paul McKaughan
Dellanna O'Brien
William O'Brien

Contents

The Authors

Paul E. McKaughan is executive director of the Evangelical Fellowship of Mission Agencies (EFMA), Atlanta, Georgia, an association of 100 U.S. mission agencies with more than 12,000 North American missionaries serving abroad. A graduate of Bethany Fellowship Bible Institute, Minneapolis, he served as a missionary in Brazil from 1962 to 1975, and from 1977 to 1987 as coordinator of Mission to the World, the foreign missions arm of the Presbyterian Church in America. He is the author of articles on the mission of the church. He and his wife, Joanne, have three adult children.

Dellanna W. O'Brien, Ed.D., is executive director of the Southern Baptist Woman's Missionary Union, Birmingham, Alabama, and is responsible for leading approximately 1.1 million women, girls and preschoolers in mission education, mission support and action, and personal witnessing. She is a graduate of Hardin-Simmons and Texas Christian Universities, and received her doctorate from Virginia Tech and State University. Prior to 1989 she was president of the International Family and Children's Educational Services in Richmond, Virginia. She and her husband, William, served as missionaries to Indonesia from 1963 to 1971. They have three adult children and six grandchildren.

William R. O'Brien is director of the Global Center, Beeson Divinity School, Samford University, Birmingham, Alabama. A graduate of Hardin-Simmons University and of Southwestern Baptist Theological Seminary, he served with his wife, Dellanna, as a missionary to Indonesia, teaching at Indonesian Baptist Theological Seminary and directing radio-television programming for Indonesian Baptists. From 1976 to 1991 he held various executive posts with the Southern Baptist Foreign Mission Board, including that of executive vice president.

Introduction

The winds of change are swirling with great intensity around the Christian missionary enterprise. The world is changing radically: economically, politically and religiously. Where does the evangelical mission community in the United States find itself in the midst of all this change?

Listen to some observers of the current mission scene.

- ❖ When did missions change from being vision-driven to budget-driven?
- ❖ Today's generation does not respond to a command structure, nor to guilt trips.
- ❖ (Mission) headquarters are afraid of decentralization.
- ❖ Most churches are interested in survival, not missions.
- ❖ The U.S. church is compassion-depleted.
- ❖ The church in America just will not listen to the church around the world.

Are these the voices of critics or cynics? Not at all. These observations are from the friends of Christian missions, persons directly involved either in churches or mission agencies.

What follows in this book comes from listening intently to scores of missions executives, church missions coordinators, theological professors and lay leaders in ten cities across America. Their commitment to the Lord Christ and to the mission of God is beyond question. Their motivation for involvement in the world Christian mission is soundly based. Why, then, do their responses give an impression that the path the missions community is on will not lead to the desired destination? Does the mere continuing existence of mission agencies guarantee effective engagement with a changing world?

As to their continued existence, when executives were asked if their agencies, or entities, went out of business would they need to be reinvented to meet real needs, they answered, "Yes." They would need to re-emerge, continuing in much the same patterns. What was never articulated was the fact that, at the operational level, the persons and entities comprising the missionary system today are thinking more about survival than the future. The future was simply a linear projection of today. There appears to be a great deal of denial about the kinds of changes that will be demanded of organizations over the next few years. Meanwhile, the stress points of change are already present.

Limited resources are one thing. But a serious stress factor is that of diminishing resources. Scarcity causes new priorities to be set and new levels of competition for what is available. Relationships between the missionaries, churches and sending structures are far more contentious now.

Another stress point comes from the changing roles of the mission agencies. Formerly they acted as mediating structures that informed their supporting constituencies about the work of their missionaries. In a sense, they were a type of buffer between poorly informed congregations and a big, threatening world where their sons and daughters were serving. And certainly they inspired churches to pray and give more for the work of those "out there" representing them.

Two Major Factors

Two of the major factors changing these structures drastically are technology and international awareness.

In the past, most information flowed through mediating structures (the mission agencies) as information moved from church to mission and back. But now, many missionaries are connected directly to churches through modern communications technology. At times, the quality and intensity of communication between church and missionary is greater and more personal than that between agency and missionary. The phenomenon can be called disintermediation. The former mediating entities are being replaced by more direct relationships between the sending churches and those sent.

In other times people in the church at home knew very little about the world "out there" beyond their limited knowledge horizon. Today, travel, international business and education have altered drastically the way people feel about the world mission field. Furthermore, education alters the way the missionary views his or her own competencies to deal with the once "exotic" peoples who inhabit today's world. The missionary now has the resources to make decisions once reserved for board administrators or church fathers.

In a world of shifting alliances, each of the components of the missions community is in quest of control—both of their own destiny, and of the environment in which world evangelization takes place. The struggles between the agencies and the churches arise from the churches seeking to reestablish meaningful participation, and escape the dominance of the agencies. The agency feels it has the expertise buttressed by years of illustrious performance and should be deferred to in terms of strategic decision making. The missionaries look at both, feeling they are the essential element and should have the right to establish priorities. After all, it is their giftedness, calling and lives that are on the line.

Too often there has been no acknowledgement that a major issue is one of power and control. Rather, the discussions get cloaked in spiritual terminology. False piety does not lend itself to candid dialogue, which can lead to deeper understanding.

It is time to take a hard look at our methods and organizational structures for Christian mission. Most of those participating in the listening groups felt the most powerful influences on the church's awareness of spiritual needs around the world are the secular media. Pastors and agency executives recognized that the media drive the attention of the local church to particular world regions and issues. They lamented the reality that if one is not working in a media "hot-spot," they are left out of the flow. Besides the secular media, Christian media figures who operate outside the mission establishments exert tremendous influence.

Jesus prayed that his followers, and all who would believe in the future, would be left in the world, not to be influenced by it, but to be transforming salt within it. With a new understanding of both our world and the commission of our Lord, we must revamp our internal training programs to equip missioners for the twenty-first century. Beyond sound theological training, our kind of world demands that we nurture the lifestyle of a servant with a humility that will listen and a selflessness that is willing to take lesser positions of power.

Lest we demand too much of the formal training centers in this matter, the real issue goes back to a renewal of the church. Every segment of the Great Commission community recognized that if renewal does not come to the church, the missions system as we know it is doomed. Continuing on its present path, the system would collapse under its own weight. And a weakened church could not carry it far into the next century.

Community at a Crossroads

The U.S. missions community is at a crossroads. Reputable and deeply committed leaders admit changes must come in our approach to mission. But all the signals indicate few are willing to make significant changes. Are we so consumed by mere survival in the present that the future does not even come up on our screen? Will there be an effective role for the North American missions community in the twenty-first century?

Given the instability of our times, such questions deserve discussion and deliberation. Therefore, this book. The pages that follow offer no single solution, no simplistic response. It is an attempt to reflect realities within the evangelical missions community, with suggestions of ways to initiate needed changes.

Resistance to the necessary changes will make for a tense future. The ability to understand the times, and know what to do about it could place the church presently in the future tense of the mission of God.

It is our prayer that God will move across our land. Even as Ezekiel witnessed a miracle in the valley of dry bones, may the drying bones of our mission structures come alive and be joined to the sinew and flesh of a new body dedicated to the establishment of Christ's rule, extending throughout all the earth.

Part One

The Context

GLOBAL REALITIES

The spirit of the twenty-first century has arrived ahead of schedule. We're used to having clocks and calendars mark the passing of time. Time is both measurable and predictable. But "the times" are not. How do you define the times? Can you take a picture of a mood, a climate, an ethos? Not really. You need a different kind of lens to see the times. Insight, intuition and imagination help illuminate the dark background of the unseen, and often the unknowable. When looking through these lenses, one realizes that the twenty-first century arrived before our calendars did. The spirit of the new millennium began working itself into the fabric of the old one in the decade of the seventies. It was like a silent, invisible invasion. It was as if a younger weaver displaced the older one at the loom, and began shaping the warp and woof of a new era. A few people began to see signs of it in the form of trends, while most of us were only caught up in fads.

Such time related aberrations should be no surprise for those of us who are involved in the world of Christian mission. After all, we claim to be involved in the timeless issue of God's purpose for the cosmos. That includes all of us. And it is time for us with the eyes of the heart to see, to understand, to interpret and to apply the kind of wisdom that begins with the fear of the Lord, and ends with a full embrace of all God is giving us to do.

First Wave

According to Alvin and Heidi Toffler in *War and Anti-War: Survival at the Dawn of the 21st Century*, we now live in a trisected world, marked by three waves of civilization. The Tofflers' First Wave was the agricultural revolution. When better food crops were produced and the means to transport that food over long distances became available, the nature of warfare changed. Troops were able to stay further afield for longer periods of time without having to stop fighting to gather food. That agricultural revolution changed the nature of life in general.

Second Wave

The Second Wave dawned with the Industrial Revolution. The first wave did not go away. It continued and coexisted with the second wave, creating a bisected world, according to the Tofflers. The emerging powers of the Second Wave were much stronger than any First-Wave power. New warfare erupted among Second-Wave powers. Even the losers in Second-Wave warfare, however, were still stronger than any First-Wave power. It was the Second Wave that brought to birth mass production, mass distribution, mass consumption, mass media and mass education. The homogeneity of the Second Wave repressed the diversity that had existed, postponing the kind of unrest that was inevitable.

Third Wave

Now we live in the midst of the Third Wave, the Information or Knowledge Age. This civilizational wave is marked by narrow-casting to particular audiences rather than broadcasting to the masses. Today, niche marketing seeks out certain kinds of buyers, not all buyers. Marketers pinpoint their advertising to small segments, not to a large, mass market. Not many vertical hierarchies are left. Rather, horizontal, flattened networks provide the means of navigation. The first two waves are ever with us. But in a trisected world, the Tofflers warn us, the most hideous wars imaginable lie ahead of us unless we find the will and the way to bypass it.

It is this trisected world that provides the context for where we must live out the agenda of God's rule and reign.

People

People and ethnic people groups occupy the central focus in the short-term future of humankind. The country or nation-state where they live no longer determines their identity. The rather new invention of nation states is undergoing its own kind of transformation. They do not play the dominant role they once enjoyed during the Second Wave. Now, tribes, clans and ethnic groupings dominate the terrain. Since the end of the Cold War, at any given moment about thirty wars are raging in different parts of the world. None of them to this point has been across a geopolitical boundary. All of them have been cultural-ethnic conflicts battling within their old Second-Wave boundaries.

Research by missiologists and ethnographers has helped us identify more than 12,000 distinct ethno-linguistic people groups. That means we can differentiate people along common ethnic and language rootage. We know where they are, whether clustered close to places of origin, or in migration throughout the world.

In *Tribes,* author Joel Kotkin describes the "tribes" that will drive twenty-first century economics. The five dominant groupings of Jews, Anglos, Chinese, Japanese and Indians transcend nationalisms in Kotkin's projections of the next century's marketplaces. In the article "Seeing Things as They Really Are," Peter Drucker goes further to say that clans within China will be the dominant economic force of the twenty-first century: "Everything is built around the clan in which all positions of influence and authority are staffed with people whom you can trust. . . . The clan culture rests on trust, not on contract."

Place

The urban setting will be home to half the world's population as we begin the next millennium. There will be over 7,000 cities with a population of more than 50,000. About 175 cities will exceed one million inhabitants. Twenty-five of those will number more than 10 million. The world's largest cities will exceed the population of many nation-states. In

Africa, urban population doubles every nine years.

The infrastructures of cities cannot keep up with that kind of in-migration. The complexity of city life is further exacerbated by the internationalization of its makeup with the presence of so many diverse ethnic groups. Every major world city is a reflection of the United Nations. When many of us were children, those who were radically different from us lived far away across oceans. Now they have moved next door. Urbanologist Ray Bakke describes the current situation as "geographic nearness with cultural distance."

Many Christians and churches in the United States do not know how to relate to their own urban reality. People have moved from rural settings to the city. They live urban, but think rural. But even those who still live in more remote areas are being urbanized if they own a satellite dish or cable television. Urban values are transmitted into the homes and minds of anyone watching television. The influence of urban realities and values is so strong that we now live out our days in an unbroken continuum between metropolitan and what we might call micropolitan, or rural.

Power

Transnational corporations are rewriting both economic theory and practice. The United Nations acknowledges about 40,000 such corporations doing business globally. The annual budgets of many of the largest corporations exceed the budgets of entire nations. The larger ones are linked by sophisticated communications systems that largely bypass the ability of federal governments to access them and know what is being said. With the technology of fiber optics, the Internet and satellite transmissions, instantaneous global transfers of funds occur every second. We live in a borderless world that is giving birth to the new city-state. In many cases it seems as if the major role left for nation-states is to play the broker between the transnationals and the city states.

Migration

The movement of people is more complex than simply shifting from the country to town. Globally there are over 100 million in migration of some kind. Almost one-fourth of these are political refugees, by the definition of the UN High Commission on Refugees. Another fourth are economic and environmental refugees. But the larger part are "intentional migrants," moving about for reasons of business, education or economic support of families back home.

It is this kind of migration, according to Ray Bakke, which causes cultural distance. This kind of migration is transforming the demographics of our neighborhoods. Whole new clusters of expatriates who have in-migrated create language and cultural enclaves that provide common language, cultural and communications lines. Such clusters conserve language, culture and tradition for the ones migrating, at least for the first generation and part of the second generation. (It is also the reason that one of every seven persons in the United States speaks another language besides English at home.) The strong cultural and religious traditions also help people resist being assimilated into their larger cultural context. Americans in general have reacted to this kind of influx; and the church in particular has been extremely slow in truly being the church in the face of this kind of opportunity.

Materialism

Materialism is the new religion of the West, if one defines religion as anything that consumes most of our time, thought and money. Some would go so far as to say that materialism is our religion, the transnational corporations are our high priests, and consumerism is our liturgy. We seem to have replaced the old Cartesian axiom, "I think, therefore I am," with a new one: "I shop, therefore I am."

The insidiousness of this religion manifests itself in the way it has penetrated into the heart of organized religion and the structural forms of Christianity. The felt need many Americans have to surround themselves with external symbols and things that become the measurement of success gets translated into corporate churchly expressions: building complexes, programs that market the church and the hoarding of human and financial resources that deprive the Good News have-nots in other parts of the world of any witness to Christ, in word or deed.

Megapoverty

Almost fifty percent of all the world's people live in poverty. The poverty scale ranges from needy to abject. The World Bank defines abject poverty as someone who lives on less than US$375 per year. Just under twenty percent of the world's population live in abject poverty (about 1 billion). The church should be concerned about all of them.

For those of us who are Christ-followers, well over 100 million of the abject poor are Christian sisters and brothers, members of our own family of faith. The acculturation of the American church means our sense of rugged individualism so influences our understanding of faith and practice that any sense of covenant accountability for the larger body of Christ is totally lost on us. It is much easier and more comfortable to privatize the faith and engage in a God-and-me mentality. (At least it is more comfortable now, this side of judgment.) The gap between haves and have-nots increases annually: material have-nots; information have-nots; Good News have-nots. In an interdependent world, the more affluent cannot buy enough insulation to protect themselves from the consequences of these inequities.

Education

In a globally interdependent world, the issue of education is critical. Lifelong learning is the only pattern that will prove effective in the present climate of continuing, rapid change. "Career" is no longer a synonym for "lifelong." People will engage in multiple careers in the course of their lives. Distance learning, collaborative group learning, on-the-job learning—these represent only a few of the options and styles that will mark twenty-first century education patterns. Even the volatile issue of population explosion is closely tied to education, or the lack thereof.

Systems that equip a person or group to think critically will have an edge over older patterns of rote learning. The old-style religious education must give way to processes that take into account how one learns, the context of that learning and the foundational need for the kind of discipling that ties together the Source of truth with every element of life, learning and application.

Environment

Ecology is not a term reserved for single-issue conservationist groups. It shares a common root with such terms as economy, ecumenical and stewardship: *oikos*, or "the household." To study, balance and manage the components of the household was a God-given task or mandate to the first humans. It is part of the comanagerial activity included in the *missio Dei* that God delegated to all of us.

- ❖ When drifting ash from the blast of Mt. Pinatubo in the Philippines falls on the Gulf of Aqaba, causing the death of coral reefs in those waters, one gets a new sense of the interdependence of all the component parts.
- ❖ The next wars in the Middle East may be over access to usable water, rather than oil.
- ❖ Global warming should not be a debate confined to competing research labs that take opposing sides on whether it is real or not.
- ❖ Bottom-line operations of corporate greed must not determine whether we inhale air that is almost chewable.

Ethics

Hardly anyone will disagree that science and technology have outdistanced our ability to think and act ethically. Nanotechnology and genetics—to name only two technologies that carry us beyond the threshold of common experience—pose major challenges to the human agenda. Everything from the human genome project to the cloning of animals reminds us that the church is far behind in giving critical attention to these topics. We seem to be revisiting the old argument of how many angels can dance on the head of a pin, while the world goes to hell in a handbasket.

CHURCHLY REALITIES

Plateau of Growth

There has been little recent conversion growth in the U.S. Protestant community. Basically, church members have engaged in musical chairs during the last two decades, moving from one church to another. Peter Wagner is quoted as saying that during the eighties, which were considered the "go-go" years for church growth in America, there was not a single county which showed a net growth in the number of evangelicals. While many megachurches grew, the source was transfer growth from other congregations that offered fewer services to parishioners. Polls indicate church attendance has remained fairly stable, with perhaps a slight decline.

Politicized

To a large degree in recent years, the U.S. evangelical community has been compromised by the Religious Right and beguiled by the promise of political power, while old-line denominations tended to identify with the political left. Many evangelicals support the politicos that share common ground on such issues as pro-family values, abortion and gay rights.

For many evangelicals, this distillation of broad public policy into a priority of the Big Three mentioned above means they have engaged in single-issue politics, at times equating godliness with a particular point of view on these issues. In so doing, we fail to recognize the degree to which our political positions have insulated us from many groups in America in desperate need. The politicization of the evangelical community has alienated us from sisters and brothers in the minority communities, especially the Black and Hispanic. Many of them may share common concerns about the issues listed above, but see the social agenda of the Religious Right as being diametrically opposed to their own interests, and to their very survival as peoples within the U.S. economic system.

Parochial

Given the overwhelming nature of global realities, the issues which have galvanized the evangelical community are local issues, a place where people feel they can get a handle on things. Business consultant Faith Popcorn coined the term "cocooning" as a characteristic of U.S. society as a whole.

In the same way, the evangelical community is cocooning into the comfortable womb of our churches. We seem to have an unprecedented

13

drive to build bigger and better salt shakers that absorb more and more resources just to maintain "the program." When we do venture out, it has more to do with local issues that relate to the political activism of the Religious Right, as a means of protecting ourselves against the encroachment of the humanists on the political left. While many issues are important, does this represent the best portrayal of Christ's concern for lost and hurting humanity?

Furthermore, we seem also to have embraced a position of international isolationism, disengaging from global issues in favor of the local. Many in the church today would not recognize the hierarchy of lostness which mission organizations have come to champion. The lost of Berkeley are just as lost as men and women in Bombay. While that may be true theologically, the issue of access to the gospel is rarely considered.

Minority

White Anglo-Saxon Protestants will become a minority in the United States during the twenty-first century. It is interesting that the only parts of the evangelical community that are growing are the minority community's churches. If one were to filter out the growth in the minority communities from denominations as notable as the Southern Baptist Convention, that denomination would show a net loss in membership over the past ten years. Three of the fastest growing churches in 1995 were minority-based churches. Worship in the United States occurs in more than one hundred languages. And the minority church community is producing mission-minded disciples. Of the more than 16,000 attending the 1996 Intervarsity Urbana Missionary Convention, almost forty percent were people of color, numerically led by the Asian contingent.

Megachurch

The megachurch has become the most influential expression of the evangelical wing of the body of Christ in the United States. This is a unique phenomenon, given that the average evangelical congregation numbers fewer than one hundred members.

Although there is a relatively small number of megachurches, their influence is spawning a new wave of quasi-connectional, or denominational relationships. Some, as in the case of Willow Creek, have formed more formal associations. Others comprise informal networks that look to one church or another for leadership, training and fellowship. Time alone will tell whether these networks become new kinds of denominations. The evidence at hand shows the influence of the megachurches far outweighs their numerical reality, either in percentage of individual membership in the evangelical community or the number of congregations when compared to the whole.

Managed

Twenty years ago it would have been difficult to find a church whose pastor had training in management. Not so today. In some instances Peter Drucker may be more frequently read by those in church leadership than are the leading theologians of the day. In U.S. evangelicalism, we "do the program." We engage in extensive research, interpret it and build the results into our programmatic activities. If today's political practitioners are guided by the polls, we in evangelical churches read assiduously the research done on society and growing churches to enable us to align ourselves with the latest findings. We talk about church members as consumers, and seek to satisfy their felt needs.

Many churches adopt a corporate model for leadership in which the session or the deacons acts as the board of directors, and the senior pastor is the CEO. Within the larger churches there may be an administrative pastor who functions as the Chief Operating Officer of the congregation. Someone has remarked if the evangelical church eliminated the Holy Spirit completely from its operation, ninety percent of the programs would continue as usual.

An overview of the evangelical church in the United States reflects a church that is politicized, plateaued and parochial; a growing minority church; the expanding influence of the megachurch; and basically a managed system. What kind of picture do we get of the mission system positioned within the evangelical world?

Mission Realities

Past its Prime

The mission system is past its prime, because many of its programs and structures are out of step with many of the world's needs and opportunities. It has also distanced itself significantly from the churches that support it. Although the spiritual needs of humankind are timeless, the contextual realities in which persons live out their existence are in constant evolution. The mission movement in America is not unlike the U.S. steel industry's decline and subsequent contraction. The world market did not stop using steel. Rather, it found other suppliers with higher quality and lower production costs because the new producers were more efficient. In spite of old U.S. ministries reaching out internationally, there are a myriad of new start-up entities emerging from local churches with entrepreneurial vision. They offer services which appear to be a better "missions buy."

Conversely, many of the old agencies are fighting to survive. Many of their programs continued long after their time of peak effectiveness. Even though many of them supply little in the way of effective ministry, they continue because people have vested interests in running them, and they find those who are still willing to support them, for whatever reason. It is as if the "missions industry" assumes that its needs are the strategic needs to be met. Organizational survival depends on the recycled visions of the past, rather than a fresh calling from the future. Past its prime, the U.S. missions community stands in need of total reconceptualization.

Ponderous

Over a period of about fifty years of continual growth, many mission agencies and ministries have specialized and proliferated. Soon after World War II, there was only one evangelical school that offered a graduate degree in missiology. Mission specialty courses in most schools were very restrictive. There were a finite number of mission boards representing the U.S. missions community, and most of them were connected with EFMA (Evangelical Fellowship of Mission Agencies) and IFMA (Interdenominational Foreign Mission Association).

Today the situation is totally different. It is hard to keep track of the number of advanced degrees in the area of mission. There are ministries and clusters of networks dealing with everything from therapy and pastoral care of missionaries, to communications and the use of sophisticated information technology. Thinly sliced and even more thinly defined specialties emerge, each with its own exclusive language and focus. Each of these ministries must draw support from the churches. The newest level of church administration—the missions pastor—is yet another dimension of cost and administration folded into the mission movement. A plethora of literature being generated is impossible for a single individual to track. In short, mission structures, networks and programs have become exceedingly complex and ponderous.

Professional

Mission has become an academic and professional discipline. Though there are many passionate people within the missions community, passion is not the word that one would use to describe missions in the U.S.A. today. We take pride and compliment one another, not for our zeal or passion, but for a much cooler and detached professionalism. The perception is that missions seems to be more of a career path, a profession, than it is a calling. We have developed our own terminology. We mainly communicate with one another within the mission community, leaving behind most of the people in the pew and many of the pastors who do not understand our technical language. In our professionalism we have become distinguished and distant from the church that supports us.

Predicting the future is impossible, and the relationship between any of these interlocking factors is complex and constantly changing. But the churchly realities are also reflected in the U.S. mission system picture. It is unrealistic to expect that the level of spirituality of missionaries will be radically different from that of the church which produces and sustains the missionary. The organizational development of the missions community is most often related directly to the corporate life of the churches and denominations from which they draw their sustenance.

The analysis presented in this book is painfully done from within the system. We who write these words are a part of the church and mission structures we talk about. We have helped develop and support many of the trends of which we are now critical. What appears to have been right at one time may have become irrelevant with the passing of time. It would be sad to realize the unwillingness to let go of past programs and structures that carried a price tag of lost effectiveness. But there is another triad of factors that reflect hope.

Renewal

There are more Christian prayer movements today in the United States than in any recent period. A decade ago organizations whose primary focus was prayer mobilization for world evangelization were scarce. Today thousands of men and women are positioning themselves to intercede for the renewal of Christ's church and revival in our nation. These renewal movements also focus on world evangelization, not just on revival in our own churches, or the restoration of this nation to its former glory. Neither is the emphasis that believers here might just be happy and satisfied in their own walk with the Lord.

Reconciliation

Billy Graham says that reconciliation is the number one issue facing the church in this country. One of the great signs of hope is that racial reconciliation has become a front-burner issue for evangelicals. For too long it has been relegated to talk, while remaining very short on action. Anglos are realizing the need to repent of attitudes of superiority and racist actions, with or without malice. Part of this quest for reconciliation arises from the realization on the part of evangelicals that they cannot divorce grace from justice for all members of our communities. As we repent and receive forgiveness, from God and from the sinned against, we can move in love. Then the world will acknowledge we are followers of Jesus Christ.

Relationship

Right relationships must extend to both persons and corporate entities. There are many signs of hope reflected in collaborative efforts among mission organizations. Such coalitions focus on the integration of all the giftedness of the body to reach particular peoples or regions. Some of the efforts are skills-based so that those engaged in Bible translation and distribution are strategizing, praying and working together to reach language groups that do not yet have the Scriptures. Other relational coalitions engage in shortwave broadcasting. They covenant, plan and work together to make sure that every language group of over one million speakers has the gospel in the heart language of the people.

These last three beacons of hope lead us to a final "R," a symbol of Christ's return. In his second epistle the apostle Peter states that there will be scoffers who will ask when and where Christ is coming. The writer admonishes in the midst of such expressed doubts, "Don't forget, God is patient and wants everyone to come to repentance." Since everything will one day be destroyed, Peter asks the question, "What kind of people are we to be?" Responding to his own rhetorical question, he answers, "We ought be people who lead holy and godly lives." And so should we live, as we look forward to the greatest sign of hope—the day of Christ's return.

Part Two

Probing U.S. Mission Realities: What We Heard

G lobal realities shape the context in which we live. Today's church and mission realities reflect the powerful influence of the global cultural context. Now we must consider some troubling questions: How much of the culture has "come to church" and quietly reshaped the church's role in serving the mission of God? Have our churchly values begun to be shaped from below, rather than from above? How does this shaping by the culture affect the vision and practice of mission agencies and entities serving as channels for those persons engaged in the mission of God? The desire to answer these questions led to a project that engaged participants in the evangelical missions community across the United States.

An initial consultation in Birmingham, Alabama, gave shape and direction to the research project (see Appendix D for a list of participants.) Subsequently, directors of the project's three sponsoring entities—Evangelical Fellowship of Mission Agencies, Woman's Missionary Union and the Global Center of Samford University's Beeson Divinity School—met with focus groups in nine U.S. cities from the Atlantic to the Pacific. Our purpose was to listen to persons directly involved in churches, agencies, seminaries and foundations who could provide candid views on a range of issues affecting the U.S. missions community.

A wrap-up consultation reconvened in Birmingham to assess the findings (see Appendix E for a list of participants.) Finally, the views expressed by participants in all nine listening conferences were clustered in seven broad categories: theological foundations, motives, church-mission relations, support, short-term missions, diversity and the shifting mission field, and structure.

THEOLOGICAL FOUNDATIONS

Mission is the crucible from which solid, relevant theology emerges. German theologian Martin Kahler stated almost ninety years ago that "mission is the mother of theology." In *Transforming Mission*, author David Bosch quotes Kahler as saying, "Theology began as an accompanying manifestation of the Christian mission." The apostle Paul expressed his theology in missionary letters to the churches he helped start.

Once theological frameworks emerge, they must be continuously assessed as to whether they remain biblically relevant, or if they have become "at ease in Zion." Mission is one way God forces us out of our theological comfort zones.

> The missionary carries his message to the frontier where Christ is not known, and finds that the message from home often does not function so well, and this leads to serious reflection. . . . This reflective process leads the missionary to look carefully at his/her own theological presuppositions.
>
> —Mission educator from Two-Thirds World

One of the first tasks of any missionary is to look all around to ascertain every evidence of the presence of God. Only then can effective contextualizing take place. In the process of contextualizing, there is always a danger of losing something important. In the face of rising pragmatism and universalism, both inside and outside the church, all the focus groups voiced the importance for theological reflection on mission to flow from God's revealed Word. Any tradeoff for relevancy or productivity would weaken the foundations. On that point one main-line evangelical leader said, "We do not want to come back in the future and discover that the theological foundations of orthodoxy must be rebuilt."

God's revealed purposes dictate that we engage in mission as a way of glorifying God. The God-centeredness of our missionary enterprise is the theological foundation on which we can build a strong edifice. Mission must be more than consumer-oriented. God is not a commodity that we can import or export. The Great Commission is not a marketing issue.

> We are not in the business of taking God anywhere as though he were some kind of commodity. The mission field isn't some dark hole to which we are bringing light. God is there and already at work.
>
> —Missionary

Theology in context must take into account the difference between personal faith and an individualistic expression of the faith. The rugged individualism of American culture undermines the issue of covenant community.

> Our individualism makes us uncomfortable with issues that are cultural, systemic and societal.
>
> —Mission professor

God addresses peoples, both in love and in judgment. In the Bible, repentance is seen as a corporate action, as well as a personal one. We need a more systemic and holistic view of mission. The community must feel an impact for justice and righteousness as a result of the presence of the body of Christ. We cannot be satisfied with the mere gathering of individuals into a church.

Reflection

Without solid theological and ecclesiological foundations, we are merely exporting a culture-driven model of church and mission. There are positive notes in terms of the influence of the churches abroad back in our own setting. Serious theological reflection in the mission context is now having an impact on churches in our own land.

For instance, the movement of prayer is cascading back into the life of the U.S. church. We can trace this development directly to the Great Commission community. It comes from the realization in many settings of what the Bible calls "a battle, not with flesh and blood, but with principalities and powers." Many churches in the U.S. realize afresh we are in the same kind of battle.

Further, from the "field" back to home has come the sense of recovering a theology of the laity. As missionaries witness firsthand the empowering of persons who have little formal education, and the outcome of their singular, impassioned commitment to Christ, it is evident that all the body of Christ is crucial to the task. From the study of Scripture it would seem it was ever so intended.

MOTIVATION FOR U.S. MISSIONS

Missionary or Mission Program?

On the surface, one might ask what is the difference between a mission program and a missionary program? Participants in the listening sessions voiced serious concerns.

> Mission-drivenness may produce missionaries. The question is whether missionary-drivenness will produce mission? Real mission-drivenness will help us escape the prison of dollars and finances, but a missionary approach may never do so.
>
> —Missions educator

> We must begin to distinguish the difference between intermediate and ultimate goals.
>
> —Missions statesman

Throughout the discussions diverse components of the evangelical missions community recognized that in the U.S. we have missionary programs, not mission programs. Much of what we have done has been built by our focus on the intermediate goal of sending missionaries. For

23

CHOOSING A FUTURE FOR U.S. MISSIONS

many, that became the end goal. If the ultimate aim is world evangelization and a worshipping community among all peoples, the assumption is that the goal would be reached by sending more missionaries. The question arises: Is our missionary-centeredness, rather than mission-centeredness, providing us a false foundation from which we do mission? Does that in any way contribute to some kind of superior role for the sent one that insidiously contributes to a spirit of triumphalism? Are the unreached of the world something to be conquered, like an enemy?

> We are thrilled when we can evangelize our enemies, such as those in the "evil empire," or the Gulf. Who will be the enemy in A.D. 2020? Do we in the U.S. need an enemy in order to marshal our forces to world evangelization?
> —Missionary on home assignment

Dare we confess that some of our past motivation for evangelization follows not from God's Word, but is enveloped by a cultural triumphalism, even a blatant technological or intellectual sense of Western superiority? One participant quoted 3 John 7, "They went out for the sake of a Name." Is our cultural triumphalism under God's judgment?

How does the Western "sending" mindset fit with the reality of thousands of new missionaries coming on line from the Southern Hemisphere? And, what is the appropriate role and response that the U.S. church can make to God's call to disciple the nations, knowing that we are not the only ones called?

Unreached Peoples and 10/40 Windows

The focus groups documented the fact that we are moving from an "unreached people" paradigm to one of discipleship. The emerging model highlights the transformational aspects of the gospel. People in the pew are thinking more holistically than ever before, even if they don't use that term. World evangelization is concerned with more than just moving a people group's name from the unreached column. Mission in today's world has to do with personal and cultural transformation.

Someone mentioned that "we are victims of our own marketing strategy." It is especially true in terms of our communication. Some viewed the "10/40 Window" as being helpful to raise the level of enthusiasm in the local church. For others, it symbolized the kind of communication that causes the eyes of persons in the pew to glaze over. It is a terminology they neither understand, nor with which they can identify. For instance:

> Today people in the church think globally, not just about missions.
>
> —Local pastor

Somehow, motivation for involvement in missions must be larger than the metaphors we use to describe it.

The perception of the location of missions and missionaries needs transforming also. The worldview that continues to perpetuate the home/foreign distinction is an impediment to a holistic vision of the world, and works against a more effective deployment of kingdom resources.

The World's Children

> We are so focused on church planting that we don't even see the children.
>
> —Missions educator

The church planting emphasis of the past 25 years helped refocus the missionary enterprise. While participants in the focus groups celebrated that fact, they also recognized the emphasis is marked by an over-simplification that has caused us to miss many of the current trends in the world today. For instance, many expressed the needed emphasis of reaching and nurturing children and youth. They represent one-half the population of all the unreached peoples of the earth. When church planting per se is both the immediate and the ultimate goal, where do children and youth fit in that construct?

Another group of children noted by the groups are those within our churches. Missions mobilizers do not see them either. We do not see the praying resources they represent, nor do we recognize that the children of major and smaller donors of today become the stewards of the next generation. These children are growing up bereft of any meaningful missions education. The missions stories of past generations do not make contact with where they are today, if they even get told.

Reflection

One cannot talk about motivation for mission separate and apart from the crucial role of the missionary. All the groups agreed that the primary role of the missionary in the future is not as a church planter. We must create a vision for missionaries to be servant-facilitators and expediters who could work with, and under, national leadership. We should do what we are good at doing. Broad categories of giftedness within the U.S. missions communities now include areas of training, planning and management. Both the shape of our corporate giftedness as Americans and the expressed needs for those gifts could shift in the next decade. But we should build our organizational purposes and visions on current realities, even as we position ourselves to be responsive to the future.

There was a contravening fear interjected into the discussions, however, that U.S. mission personnel might just become theorists and supporters, and not actual doers of ministry. If we abdicate our responsibility on the issue of sharing the Good News of Jesus Christ, we would become technocrats rather than persons sharing where to find water in a dry and thirsty world.

THE TRIANGLE:
CHURCH - MISSION AGENCY - MISSIONARY RELATIONS

The issue generating more discussion than any other was that of church - mission - agency - missionary relationships. There seems to be a whole new focus on ecclesiology as it relates to the local church. It was almost a rule that when anyone spoke of the church, it was the local congregation being discussed, rather than the body of Christ at large. Like a domino effect, this focus touches the other dimensions of agency and missionary.

The Local Church

> The mission train is being pulled by a new engine: the local church.
>
> —Former missionary, now a mission pastor in local church

> The local church is the beginning and the ending of everything in missions.
>
> —Local pastor

> The local church doesn't need to be told what to do, but it needs to be helped by the missions agencies to do what she wants to do.
>
> —Local pastor

A new day in missions and local church relationships has dawned, and the sun is high in the sky. Those sensing this reality are saying that mission agencies had better come to terms with this new development. The local churches express their desire to be the dominant partners in any relationship between church and agency. The local body feels that financial and human resources are theirs, and there is a stewardship responsibility to make sure they are getting the most effective returns on all of it.

In the emerging push-pull of this relationship, the question arises as to who exists to serve whose purpose? But there is no misunderstanding that the center of gravity in missions has moved from the agency to the local church, and that churches would no longer be passive contributors to someone else's vision. Even those church leaders who supported agencies in the more traditional mode stated their desire to become much more proactive in the relationship.

Even among the most responsive agencies, there are downsides to such new relationships. Mission leaders expressed frustration over the reality that when their agencies have geared up to serve the vision of a church, there may have been a shift in leadership or a change of focus within the church that left the agency holding the bag. Another frustration emerges when agencies are asked to customize programs to fit the dream of the churches, and at the same time asked to lower their cost of doing the customizing business.

Another tension point comes with the agency's loss of authority as a go-between. The globalization of trade, the use of communication technology, ease of travel and the short-term experience all combine to undermine the intermediary role of the agency between the mission field and the local church. Members of local congregations travel the world for business and pleasure. Somehow, these congregational communicators seem more trustworthy than the professional go-betweens.

Among local churches, there is great disparity between large and small. The capacity of the larger churches to do their thing ranges from being their own sending agencies to establishing partnerships with entities that could resource the churches. One perspective:

> Depending on the vision of the pastor, in the future the megachurch will be a sending agency. They will get a lot less attention from the agencies because they will be one.
>
> —Missions mobilizer

There were mixed signals from the smaller church arenas. On the one hand:

> Small churches are overwhelmed by the complexity of adopt-a-people programs.
>
> —A layperson

On the other hand, one who spoke of small churches stated:

> The missions [agencies] are under-challenging the small churches. The agency of my denomination asked my church to give them $300 per month, when our budget as a small church of 250 members was $300,000 per year for foreign missions.
>
> —Local pastor

In all the small church diversity, there was a strong feeling that the largest untapped reservoir for mission was the small church, and that these churches were not reaching their potential as participants in the Great Commission community.

One further reaction from all kinds of churches, especially those with gifted members who want to be involved, relates to "sheep stealing."

> The church has become a shell since the activists have been siphoned off by the parachurch ministries. They want to minister out there where it is exciting, not in the local setting. The person in the local church must be nurtured, and not just picked green by the parachurch ministries.
>
> —Missions pastor in a local church

There is a strong backlash in the local churches where they perceive themselves as producing effective disciples, and then see the most gifted siphoned off for a ministry other than their own. In this context, agencies are seen as taking from the church, instead of adding effectiveness to the ministry of the church. Strained relationships serve no one.

The Mission Agency

Intense discussions about missions agencies included old patterns—the way it has been—along with current realities and future should be perspectives.

> There has been an implied "just let us do it" mentality that denotes a certain kind of arrogance on the part of the agency which really didn't listen.
>
> —Mission executive

From the other side of the road:

> Those who come in throw the grenade into the crowd and run.
>
> —Local pastor

Both the "just let us do it," and the "throw the grenade into the crowd" are two perceptions of the same reality. In the past, the agency felt it had a corner on the market, and the church existed to support the vision of the missions expert. The agency came to the church periodically to stir up the fire for the vision, with the hope of producing more missionaries and money.

That day is over. Any attempt to project it into the future will lead to obsolescence for the agency, and force the church into a more exclusive role.

> We missions agencies must break out of this control thing. The church controls the actions. "Boomers" don't want to write checks. They want to be involved in missions strategies, . . . in the process. But this process must be tangible. The local church is taking back control from the agency.
>
> —Mission executive

The fear of being marginalized is causing a lot of soul-searching within agencies. The same dynamic is also causing changes within the church community. Those responsible for missions within the local congregation know that if the missions program is not more relevant, it will die.

> The role of the missions agency has changed from being the "doer" of missions to being the "facilitator" of local churches.
>
> —Local church laity

Yet another voice:

> Missions agencies are becoming more coordinating agencies for [individuals] in local churches that want to do something for God. In reality, we don't have control. We bemoan it at times. But, the people in the pew are redefining what missions means, and these people will go elsewhere if we don't change to meet their desires.
>
> —Megachurch pastor

Most missionaries probably feel they are the "doers" in missions. Most missions agencies feel that is their area of expertise. But agencies on the cutting edge recognize that ministry belongs to the church. God gave the responsibility for world evangelization to all the church.

The biggest challenge we face for the future is the issue of learning to listen to the local church—a local church which many times just doesn't understand.

—Mission executive

Churches today would answer that missions executive, "Whose fault is it that we don't understand?" Why hasn't the mission agency taught them to be active participants, to be involved in shaping policies, rather than expecting deference to a group of experts enshrined in an agency office somewhere?

Giving up control of the process is hard, especially when one's whole life has been devoted to understanding the world. Agencies are changing. But many executives feel whipsawed between field personnel who have sweat equity in their agency's work and do not see the need for change, and the local churches who demand constraints of overhead from the agencies.

There is another new dimension to the issue of control.

We are in a missiological shift and have been sucked into all this gen-erational stuff. We have to look at people who need the Lord, people here at home who have to change their life and worldview. We as missions people need to re-evangelize the United States.

—Mission executive

Without question, mission agencies will dedicate many more resources to work within our own geographic boundaries. The work will face two directions: the local church itself, and the world's population that have come to our shores. This will affect the way an agency promotes itself.

Mission agencies must reposition themselves. It is more than packag-ing. People don't respond to our mission. Advertise a seminar on mis-sions in the Sunday School, and you will be the only people there, except for a few old folks.

—Missionary

For most of our history it was the agency experts and the missionaries who knew what was going on "over there." But with the mobility of this generation, it is no longer the case that knowledgeable people are restricted to agencies. Mission agencies are under the same scrutiny as that of local ministries. The following statements reflect this point-counterpoint.

> Slick promotional material many times doesn't have ministry backup. Our local church people are supporting things that are not productive.
> —Mission mobilizer

> That may be the case, but this disconnect won't work any longer, because the people are going out there to look for themselves.
> —Local laity

Our promotional material must match the realities that will be examined by supporters and friends, as well as those in local churches looking for ways to increase the effectiveness of their missions dollars.

Where does the mission agency fit in the emerging paradigm, and what will it take to communicate more effectively within the context of churches? When the game changes, and the field of play changes, the rules change also. We now need both a new vocabulary and a new image undergirding the world Christian mission.

We can no longer assume the person in the pew understands the language of mission from a past era. Local churches and agencies must put some effort into determining how God's design for all the peoples of the world makes sense to the average follower of Christ.

Along with a new vocabulary, we must shape a new mythology of mission as well. Myths are important. They capture and communicate the values that people hold dear and want to emulate. Most older missions biographies are a long way from the daily life of the average North American Christian. Professional mission personnel, in collaboration with local church leaders, could certainly help influence new understandings, with a vocabulary to undergird them.

But, the agency still faces a challenge as to its own identity and role.

> We work with the church, but we have a theological problem. As mem-
> bers of the body of Christ we are not considered a legitimate part of
> the church. The local church places itself at the center of the church.
> We who are called "parachurch ministries" are placed at the margin,
> when acknowledged at all.
>
> —CEO of a parachurch ministry

Not wanting to alienate powerful voices from the local churches, one
said:

> We have always seen ourselves as an apostolic team. In a sense, we have
> been recognized by the local church, but are not governed by them.
>
> —Mission executive

Living within these pressures, even agency leaders acknowledge that
as mission boards "we have not done much of our ministry as real servants, here or there." In the light of current realities, many leaders admit
that in the future they will be minority players, and will be forced to
serve.

Meanwhile, other pressures are closing in.

> In the future we may not be allowed to continue at the financial or
> personnel levels we enjoy today. We may have to scale down as the
> culture from which we do missions changes and becomes less sup-
> portive.
>
> —Mission executive

Missions will have fewer career people, more lay people, more bivo-
cational persons, with a preponderance of short-term personnel. This
new model will have to re-engineer roles, and think much more about the
application of spiritual giftedness alongside that of indigenous leaders,
both in this country and abroad. And that comes back to the stewardship
of resources.

> You missions agencies can provide essential linkage to the credible
> leaders in other countries with those of us who want to support them.

> You agencies have to rethink how you use money. I [speaking of a foundation] will support people who I cannot control if I trust them. But, I can't tell people what they need or don't need—even here, much less in another country.
>
> —Grant-making foundation executive

There is a facilitating role that global mission agencies will play in the future. But, in shifting to a facilitating and consulting role from former primary operational roles, there is another concern.

> I am concerned that we degenerate into a U.S. mission culture where we pay someone else to do what we should be doing. Missions is becoming incredibly more complex with this shift in roles.
>
> —Missionary

The Missionary

The "doer," the one who supplies the sweat equity, now experiences an identity crisis in terms of the future.

> The biggest issue we face is not the decrease of the missionary force, but the role of the missionary. Where do they fit in the Great Commission?
>
> —Mission executive

And a little different slant:

> We feel the national church could do a better job of church planting, but our agency is married to missionaries.
>
> —Mission executive

When being true to biblical models, there will always be those apostolic teams in the Pauline tradition who go where no church exists. Inevitably, this will involve North American missionaries. But, there is a growing recognition that the price of supporting the North American models is too high, even when scaled down from their counterparts back home.

Beyond awkwardness in serving from an affluent platform in contexts quite different from those in the West, there is another awkwardness forcing itself in upon us.

> North American missionaries are not prepared to handle the unprecedented growth of the church that is taking place around the world.
> —Former missionary now a mission pastor in local church

That pastor went on to explain that many times North Americans fear that kind of explosive growth, and tend to slow it down so they can consolidate, rather than fuel the fire of God's Spirit in the midst of explosive growth. One hopes that the adaptability of North American missionaries will rise to adjust to the new realities of strong churches in the Two-Thirds World and their own involvement in world mission, often at much greater financial sacrifice than that paid by those from the West.

> The whole relationship between missionary and national has to change. We used to talk about looking for our "Timothys." This is no longer viable. In many instances, the U.S. missionary will be the "Timothy," and the national leader the "Paul."
> —Missionary

The Holy Spirit has taught these "Pauls" lessons through persecution and suffering that bring new and deeper levels of maturity often lacking in our own national cocoon of ecclesiastical self-indulgence. Any new missions mythology must be developed around servanthood, humility, and new relationships of power with national churches:

> We have to subordinate our goals. . . . We need to be willing to be equippers, . . . to come alongside. That is a completely different mindset. We have been in control so long that it seems natural. We fail to recognize that the Holy Spirit distributes gifts within the body as he wills. And, the gifts of the Spirit are not the prerogatives of the educated, not the prerogatives of skin color or even historic mission tradition.
> —Mission executive

Reflection

In thinking through all that has been said, it is obvious that the three component parts of the missions triangle present an increasingly complex picture for the future role of the U.S. missions community. The patterns of local church initiatives represent more than a blip on the screen of church history. It will be interesting to see what new relationships emerge between churches, missionaries and the agencies that learn new ways to service both churches and missionaries.

A fourth component only alluded to in this section is that of the donor base for missions. Given the rising disparity between the elements of the mission triangle, the reality of the disconnectedness of the donor base from all the other components further complicates the picture. Sympathetic foundations that have traditionally funded much of the agencies' work are now functioning as a network of peers that is shaping its own missiological priorities. A major challenge for the future is finding the ways these four components can work more collaboratively.

MISSION SUPPORT

Money and financial affairs bring to high visibility the tensions and competitive spirit between various components of the missions community. Agencies know that opportunities outstrip resources. Churches feel they are bombarded with requests for more money. Agencies know that our churches have resources far beyond those of the church in any other part of the world, or at any other point in human history. At times, church leaders complain about the lack of careful use of those funds on the part of mission executives and missionaries.

Whose Resources?

> Our church was assaulted by more than 650 requests for money in this past year.
>
> —Missions pastor in local church

> I want the church to be missions-minded, not just missions generous.
>
> —Pastor

> There is a great disconnect between the mission agency and the church, many times in the area of finance.
>
> —Laity

> You say you want to be servants to us, yet no communication ever comes to us or our people without a return envelope. What kind of help is that?
>
> —Pastor

It became apparent in discussions that often the church does not use the same yardstick for evaluating its own programs. It seems to underreport overhead and overreport results, just as the mission agencies are accused of doing. There is another kind of drama going on within the local church reflected in a statement with a two-way mirror.

> The local church must determine what God is telling them to do as stewards of God's resources.
>
> —Pastor

This comment was not just aimed at mission agencies. It also referred to members of the congregations supporting activities not condoned by the church. Those in authority or those elected to care for the church's assets complain when persons, or groups, within the church exercise the same freedom of choice that the church exercises vis-a-vis the mission agencies. The shift of financial control and a sacred consumer activism is hitting the local congregation just as it is the mission agencies.

Financial Limits

> We can't take care of the support of the people from our own congregations that the mobilizers have stirred up to go overseas.
>
> —Local missions pastor

That expression of frustration is coupled with another built-in conflict.

> Our church is tired of seeing the shiny young mission candidate's face that hasn't done anything. Our people want to support those who have core competencies, that have been proved.
>
> —Missions committee member

Contrast that statement with a different frustration.

> Our church is encountering difficulty raising the support for those who are on the field.
>
> —Missions pastor

The tensions and frustrations caused by limited resources are equally felt by churches and agencies. Beyond the good-natured and not so good-natured complaining done by pastors and agency executives, there was a growing consensus.

> We have to stop marketing and start manufacturing churches that have the right missions genes.
>
> —Missions educator

> Many of the problems we are facing financially come from the fact that both mission agencies and churches are so busy marketing that they are not giving adequate attention to really building, creating, cultivating the appropriate seedbed for giving, not only now, but especially for the future.
>
> —Pastor

Foundations and Major Donors

> Foundations will increasingly exert influence on the missions movement, and they seem to be narrowing their focus.
>
> —First generation immigrant in ethnic church

Foundations and major donors are the most rapidly growing component of mission funding. For the first time, foundations are banding together to determine what will or will not be funded. Unfortunately, much of the discussion goes on without the input of thinkers from the operational missions world. The situation grows more complex related to perspectives internal to the foundation's operation.

> Foundation staff and foundation principals tend to operate under a different motivation. The former tend to be cynical because they deal with mountains of proposals, many times not backed with perceived performance. The latter are those who founded the entity, and engage with providing it with resources. They tend to be motivated by vision and dreams of making a difference for Christ's kingdom.
> —Board chair of a foundation

The "quick fix" mentality for all kinds of problems is not the sole possession of an impatient secular public.

> We have a major problem in missions, because the major donors want what missionaries cannot produce. They want quick results.
> —Woman mobilizer for giving

Many of those involved as major donors are from the business world where life fluctuates with the quarterly report. They want a similar kind of measurability in the missions world, and the same kind of growth as that expected in commercial enterprises. Minimally, they want to see mission agencies exercise more discipline in evaluating results. The same mobilizer quoted above said, "The wealthy don't mind risk; they understand it. But, in this risk process there must be accountability."

Those who trumpet their plans must understand that donors will not continue to provide support to ministries that obscure their performance.

New Sources

Beyond foundations and major donors, in the traditional sense, there were other sources of funding that were discussed in the focus groups.

> The missions movement must look to the U.S. ethnic communities for financing. They are getting rich, and they go unchallenged with world

evangelization. They are progressing because they are more resource-
ful than the Anglos.

—First generation immigrant

The next few years will see the largest generational transfer of wealth
in the history of this country: approximately $15 trillion.

> Missions is not taking seriously the generational transfer of wealth,
> much of it to women. They are not on our development teams or our
> boards of directors.
>
> —Woman educator

Three Big Questions

> Are we in the U.S. building mission structures that can't possibly be
> maintained in the future?
>
> —Laity

Both agency and church leaders feel the missions system has
become too complex. Some strategic abandonment of significant por-
tions of our programmatic baggage would free up resources for new or
more relevant Great Commission ventures.

> As financing becomes international, who is going to insist on being
> the quarterback? Who calls the plays becomes a big issue.
>
> —Mission executive

This is not a hypothetical question in a world where regions like Asia
play a much larger role in the funding of Christian mission. In places like
Korea and Singapore, there is new money not already committed like
funds in this country. Will they follow the older, more paternal model of
controlling every aspect of funding?

> Money follows people, individuals. And, this personalization of
> finances makes collaboration the true last frontier in missions.
>
> —Missions educator

The vast amount of money given in support of missions from North America is tied to people—"our kind of people." This reality undergirds the perspective that we are more in the missionary business than in the business of mission. Ever-larger amounts of money are needed to support a Western-style missionary operation. If the cost of doing missions U.S.-style is so great, absorbing our present resource base, how do we create new pools of money with which to collaborate with the new wave of cross-cultural missionaries from new sending countries throughout the southern hemisphere?

Reflection

There was common recognition by all segments of the U.S. missions community that the cost of doing mission by North Americans has risen to the point of almost pricing us out of the market. We have moved from a labor-intensive ministry to a capital-intensive ministry. While this may not be the whole issue, missiologically speaking, we must exercise much greater stewardship of all our resources.

Another clear signal was the uniform discontent with the present deputation system. Missionaries tend to view "support raising" as a kind of unpleasantness they must endure to do what God has called them to do. The local churches do not like the system because it divides the missionary in small pieces and dilutes the ability of the church to make personal identification and accountability practical. Agencies are not totally enamored with the system either. But, aside from denominational support systems that guarantee the underwriting of missionary support, no one has yet come up with an alternative approach.

Collaboration with Two-Thirds World churches and their mission endeavors clearly remains as a major challenge to all concerned. Can we find a way to present to the unbelieving world the face of unity? Is the role of finances a place to start? After all, Jesus reminded us that where our treasure is, there will our hearts be also.

SHORT-TERM MISSIONS

Short-term mission involvement claimed much of the discussion in all the focus groups across the nation. Its importance directly relates to the priority local churches are giving to it.

> Short-term mission is the only hope for future involvement in missions because presently eighty percent of mission support comes from a generation that is dying off. Short-terms are bringing back the excitement in missions.
>
> —Pastor

> The only hope for the compassion-depleted church is short-term missions.
>
> —Boomer Generation leader

Both the churches and those engaged in short-term endeavors articulate a theological and methodological assumption: "Since Christ and Paul used this methodology, we should accept it with open arms." Yet tradition and professional mission entities resist short-term missions. Career missionaries often view it as "baby-sitting," while many in the local church are concerned that short-term work becomes merely "vacations with a purpose."

Who is going on short-term mission projects? Almost everyone, from youth to the aging. There is an interesting trend among adults:

> Short-terms for us is moving toward a family involvement. A father doesn't want to spend all of his vacation away from his kids.
>
> —Buster Generation leader

More family involvement may be on the growing edge of the short-term movement.

Elements for Effectiveness

> At our school, sixty-five percent of the incoming students have had a short-term experience; forty percent have been overseas more than

once. The question arises, what is the difference between short-term missions and field trips in high school? How does one distinguish the latter from real missions? Many times our students don't know the difference.

—Missions educator

In focus group discussions, the difference between short-term missions and the typical field trip seemed to be in pre-field discipleship training. One mission pastor in a large church felt that the preparatory phase became the most highly leveraged discipleship opportunity that his church had. This church placed a moratorium on short-term programs until they could develop an adequate training program for leaders and participants. By their own admission, the difference before and after was that of night and day.

A second element contributing to effectiveness is the interface of the short-term missionary team with committed nationals in the field. Comparisons of lifestyle, commitment and effectiveness in ministry could be highlighted. Processing and understanding the experience in the midst of it also made it more meaningful back in the home setting.

A vital element is an adequate debriefing of the experience upon the return home. This includes what to do with lessons learned while on the trip. Furthermore, it deals with how commitments made in the compressed crucible of communal life and foreign experiences can be turned from good intentions into reality.

Relation of Short to Long

We might develop a farm system for missions where people start out doing short-term missions, and then become part of a kind of intermediate mission, and then finally at a later stage become full-fledged missionaries.

—Missions elder

With no intention of implying levels of spirituality in the developing stages mentioned above, there is a new wave of missions within the church that is not necessarily short-term at all. For instance, at the "corporate" level of church, we are seeing long-term involvement lived out in short bursts. One church has worked for eight years at a particular site in Mexico City. While utilizing different short-term volunteers over the eight years, the relationship has become long-term. Another church has a long-term relationship in Bosnia, but cycles various members of the church into the area for three-month, and shorter, time periods. Over seventy percent of the membership has been involved in brief periods in Bosnia in this long-term relationship. They have developed sophisticated ways to transfer relationships from one short-term group to the next.

Two major agencies, Youth With A Mission and Operation Mobilization, provide examples of short-term ministries turning into long-term missions involvement. YWAM has become the largest long-term agency in the world, even though it may engage 100,000 persons a year in short-term projects. OM now has long-term presence in many parts of the world.

At another level, agencies are finding that many of their long-term missionary candidates had been involved in multiple short-term experiences before committing themselves to vocational missions.

Pitfalls to Avoid

> Short-term mission fortifies the American's superiority complex. It builds on our "can-do-anything" mentality.
>
> —Mission executive

In the listening sessions continual emphasis was given to the need to be servant oriented and to avoid an attitude of triumphalism. Often, unrealistic expectations are created by those going out, and by those receiving them. Some who are hosts of these short-termers with "superior education and economic status" may expect veritable miracles. It is a temptation to accept this somewhat exalted state and fail to realize one's limitations.

In our relational world, it takes years to build real relationships. Short-terms are problematic, since it presupposes that a relationship can be built in a short period of time.

—Missionary on furlough

Not only is this a problem in very difficult and sometimes dangerous parts of the world, but it also runs the risk of trying to telescope into an intense relationship what normally takes years to accomplish. Expectations created in that brief timeframe easily go unmet, bringing with it some very regrettable fallout.

With all the short-term missionaries, and the ratio of short-term to long-term missionaries going out from America, you have to change the job descriptions and the expectations of what can be accomplished.

—Missions executive

Short-term missions has had and will continue to have a profound impact on the overall missionary enterprise in North America. To ignore it, or to resist it, is a form of nearsightedness that has fatal flaws. Many congregations have been "out there" and have seen firsthand what is going on. They have been impressed by the commitment of Christ-followers who have far less materially and have paid a greater price for their faith. We must avoid the pitfall of a "we-they" mentality within the missions enterprise.

Reflection

Short-term missions is one of the demythologizing forces that has removed mission from its exalted status in the home church. The expectations of those involved are high. Perceived benefits for the churches and the participants in the short-term experience are what drive this phenomenon. When at their best, short-term projects build on the foundations of the career model. In many instances, without the work of the long-term precursors the shorter experience would not have been viable.

Whatever one's perspective, the trend toward the short-term engagement is here to stay, and will alter the way we do mission in the twenty-first century.

DIVERSITY AND THE SHIFTING MISSION FIELD

> We give intellectual assent to mutual giftedness, but we don't know
> who we are, or what we are gifted to do.
> —Leader of sports outreach ministry

Mutual—and very diverse—giftedness. In all the discussions about diversity, the issues basically fell out along three lines: generational, ethnic and gender.

Generational

"Gen X," "Baby Busters," "20-Somethings" are labels for a generation that abhors being labeled.

> A "Buster" is one who has many options, and wants to keep them all
> open.... This generation feels it knows nothing, and so it can question
> everything. . . . This generation will do anything as long as you do it
> with them. . . . People need an invitation to be on mission with God,
> not guilt trips.
> —Buster Generation leader

So speaks one of the mission leaders from within that age group. Representatives from this generation were few and far between in our listening sessions. Nevertheless, their contributions cast new light on the discussions, and were clearly distinctive from the insights of other generational cohorts participating.

They were not interested in the large, worldwide programs. Rather, they wanted to deal more intimately and in depth with small groups. Through building relationships and discipleship they would have an impact, rather than building on promises around large programmatic initiatives. They have a strong commitment to unreached people, but seemed not to accept the hierarchy of unreached peoples posed by previous generations. To them there is no great distinction between "here" and "there." This group assumed word and deed ministries to be one together, and of equal importance. Further, assumptions in the discussions reflected on the reticence of the "20-Somethings" to work in institutions run by and for the "Silent Generation." This younger group will probably form their own institutions. The bottom line:

> This present generation wants to make a difference, but we will have to sell them in very different ways on world evangelization.
>
> —Pastor and prayer mobilizer

"Selling them" is not simply a marketing problem. It goes to the very ethos of our organizational structure.

Builders and Boomers

> Baby Boomers and those of the Silent Generation have things to say in missions, and they will say them because of their sheer numbers as they move into retirement and volunteerism.
>
> —Pastor

Significant numbers of people are moving into mission in the midst of career changes. Persons in their forties and fifties are taking early retirement, moving from "success to significance," in the words of Bob Buford, founder of the Leadership Network. These people will set the organizational tenor of our mission agencies for a period of time as they seem to be gravitating toward established mission structures.

There will also be tensions brought into the situation. For instance, the Builder Generation admires those who have been living out a lifetime of commitment in mission, but harbors deep reservations for Baby Boomers, tending to see them as somewhat superficial. When mission organizations try to mix the oil and water of the younger generational cohort with that of their immediate predecessors moving into second careers, there is a significant clash of values. Values differ within the various groups.

> Our fellowship is going through a generational shift, and this brings ethnic challenges directly into the mix.
>
> —Local pastor

It was evident in all the discussions that both the Boomers and the 20-Somethings were bringing ethnic differences and racial reconciliation directly onto the evangelical radar screen. Boomers sense the need to fix the problem older generations had swept under the rug. The younger cohort see it at a more personal level, wanting to live out Christ's love for all people in tangible ways.

Ethnic Diversity

> We don't even know what we look like as the U.S. body of Christ. We may reinvent ourselves out of a false identity.
>
> —Ethnic pastor

In the evangelical missions community, those still dominating in leadership are primarily "male, pale and aging." Missions in the future cannot maintain this status quo. In contrast, the growing edges of the evangelical church are within the ethnic communities, while the Anglo church has plateaued, or is already in decline. Much of this has happened while white evangelicals have tended to escape into foreign missions, avoiding the racial divides that exist in America.

Blacks and ethnic groups are barely represented, if at all, on boards and in places of leadership in the traditional evangelical missions community. That reality was reflected in their very small number of representatives among all the focus groups. To ignore this fact much longer will continue to erode the credibility of the enterprise, while destroying any potential for unity.

> Racial divisions will lead to the "Balkanization of America," and only the church stands in the way with a moral position to do something about it.
>
> —Ethnic church mobilizer

And a flood of expressions emerged:

> When will we as white males speak up for the type of integration and giving up our prerogatives that will be necessary to move from a white

male dominated society to true diversity?

—White leader

We have allowed our racism and tribalism to push us into our present situation. In our trying to deal with world evangelization from here in the U.S. we are trying to maintain some kind of supremacy in missions.

—Black pastor

We want to add color to our ministries. But, are we thinking about the older paradigm of color? Or, are we really going to recognize our ethnocentrism and work across the divisions to the formation of a real consortia?

—Ethnic church mobilizer

In a particularly poignant moment when the issue of fear, suspicion and angry white males brought to sharp focus the ferment generated by the issue, a woman directly challenged the group, and especially the white males.

When will it be done? Who is going to do it so that my heart can be quiet? I want you men to do this, men whom I trust so that I can rest.
—Black woman theological educator

There may be untapped resources within our ranks that can bring new insight to the question.

Are we fighting a battle that the kids have already dealt with? Are we fighting the wrong battle, are we late, too late, in dealing with this issue for our generation?
—Pastor and father of a 20-Something young adult

There is a recognition that the Buster Generation has experienced a major shift in race relations. Perhaps they can lead their elders so as not to merely fight old battles in old ways.

Gender

One of the big surprises in the listening exercise was either the unwillingness or the inability of the participants to deal with issues surrounding gender diversity. There was a bit more comfort in dealing with generational and ethnic issues. Sometimes the topic was like a parenthesis or a postscript to the "real" issues being discussed, and even then it was usually a woman who had to introduce the subject. White males comprised the majority of the groups. They certainly knew that modern missions history is replete with the stories of effective women who carried the weight of the enterprise. Those same men knew that women control much of the financial resources.

> What are we going to do when we go into China and find that sixty-seven percent of the pastors are women, and we in missions only have male leaders? A lot of ministries in churches may have to adjust their theology.
>
> —Woman missions leader

Women are growing angry as they sense they have been marginalized from meaningful roles in world evangelization.

> We put people in so many different and confining boxes. They can't get out of their boxes to minister. These are boxes of tradition, custom, training, gender, and even race and language.
>
> —Woman in child ministry

If those in positions of power do not deal with this issue, we believe there will be a new revival of women's structures within the church. These will be competitive mission-sending structures and women-support structures.

The omission of women from every level of the world mission enterprise spells a failure to include the greatest unused resource at the disposal of the U.S. church in its cross-cultural quest to reach the world.

Where Is the Mission Field?

One of God's gifts to the church in America for world evangelization is the "stranger among us." Many of the unreached people groups of the world are now present in the United States and Canada.

> The church in America must come to terms with the "Samaritans" living among us.
>
> —Missions educator

> In a ten block radius of my church there are over 50,000 workers with whom we are engaged in citizenship training, language learning. We are working with internationals as a missions extension.
>
> —Pastor

> In our city there are 90 languages in the school system, and 60 unreached people groups. The division between "here" and "there" is superficial.
>
> —Pastor

The influx of people from every part of the globe was cited as the biggest reason for reorienting the whole missionary enterprise. We must cast aside the boundaries of "here" and "there." Many expressed the need to "redefine Jerusalem," moving from that base rather than merely taking gigantic geographic leaps.

With cross-cultural realities and the gift of multiculturalism, there is the new challenge of the internationalization of Christian missions. Those groups who have already engaged in cross-cultural mission teams admit the difficulties that go along with the ideal. One leader raised the difficult question as to whether people really want to integrate to serve the cause. Will it be that only our leaders can interface? This question was on a generational level that points out that people tend to work together with a cohort of individuals they understand.

When the playing field changes, and the game changes, so do the rules. The ultimate solution lies in the truth that "unless a grain of wheat falls into the ground and dies, it remains alone." Who will be willing to die to the times and realities that no longer exist?

Reflections

Uniformity or unity? Until the church comes to peace with the diversity of God's creation, and the purpose behind that diversity, divisiveness will be the hallmark by which we are known. If there is a connection between love and unity, we must be willing to engage the issues of ethnicity, gender and generation.

Global migration will guarantee the church cannot get off the hook lightly. Where we go and who takes the lead is not nearly so important as whose we are, and how we serve.

STRUCTURAL ISSUES FOR THE FUTURE

We are moving from an organizational paradigm of order and control which was derived from the Industrial Age. The new information era into which we have moved will be administratively much less neat. Where once our structures tended to dominate and control, now structures will be much more subservient to our task. The silos of our organizational divisions will give way to an interchange between them as their walls are broken down. Seemingly unrelated factors contribute to the reordering of structure.

> Many new missionaries are not on anybody's list. They can't get on them because they are working outside the system.
>
> —Local pastor

> Rapidly growing movements like Youth With A Mission and Operation Mobilization are systemically messy. The only thing that holds them together are their values, their vision and their covenantal relationship. OM has 80 different organizations within it, and 40 of them [are] unincorporated.
>
> —Parachurch mission executive

> In 2020 there will be a lot of duplication of efforts. The teams of Boomers and Busters will impact the missions world in ways we can't even envision. The sovereign God in heaven will be coordinating zillions of new movements. It will be like standing on an anthill wondering who has ordered the apparent chaos, but in fact it is

coordinated. It looks confusing; it looks like waste; but it is quite effective.

—Younger mobilizer

None of the groups predicted a future in which organizational definition or control would be simpler than today. All of us will have to cultivate a gift for ambiguity, and the ability to function without precise definitions, even if fuzzy patterns look like waste.

> What we might call waste may look different from the perspective of God. The salmon procreation process would appear to be a wasteful way of continuing the species, but a whole lot of biological systems are sustained by this waste.
>
> —Prayer movement leader

There seems to be a growing impatience with any definition of diversity as a license for independence. And, there is a negative backlash with movements or groups that are self-serving. World problems and tightening resources force us to be better stewards in an interdependent relationship.

We may see clusters of micro-ministries emerge, growing into constellations of networks that are interrelated by information technology, enhancing those joined in common cause. Discussions focused on cooperative ventures larger than one organization could envision.

> We need a generic structure that will formulate the "Got Milk?" ads for the missions movement. No one agency is big enough to do that. We would need to do it together.
>
> —Mission executive

All of this underscores the need for collaboration to become the norm, rather than our individualism.

Meanwhile, if the missions community continues to ignore the need for profound structural changes in its modus operandi, the generation that is moving into the dominant role of supply and demand in the area of power and finances for world evangelization will increasingly ignore us in turn. There is a truism: The Baby Boomer fights the institution; the Buster just ignores it.

Downsizing or Right-sizing?

An undercurrent running through the discussions reflected different perceptions on the part of churches and missions agencies. While the mission organization was anticipating expansion, churches were saying the funds for expansion are limited. Money for the right kind of personnel is increasingly tight. Structures could well be facing a significant period of downsizing. Would that be all wrong?

> Structures are built, and as they grow they become more dominant. It is a deceptive thing. How will the Two-Thirds World mission agencies relate to our expensive Western structures? They want to work with us without having to accumulate all of the organizational trappings we have.
>
> —Mission executive

With the past generation, which so faithfully supported missions, passing on, we have the opportunity to do what we presently do with less money (if all we're doing deserves to continue). We need to turn to our lay people for answers on the "how-to."

> We need to think about doing the same job with fewer people, not just adding to the head count. When you downsize, you magnify the importance of relationships.
>
> —Laity

Big may not be as beautiful in the future.

Reflection

Most organizations continue to add programs, while being reluctant to terminate marginal, or no longer effective, ones. Peter Drucker reminds us that the main reason that new initiatives fail is that they are put in direct competition with program initiatives that are mature. He dares to suggest the best way to renew an organization is to discontinue a program or product every time a new one is added. Consensus among those in the listening sessions revealed the need for missions organizations to reconsider the relationship between size and purpose. If not yet a massive movement within mission organizations, there are the vibrations of a ground swell in the making.

> I am optimistic about what God is doing in missions. There is a positive side to the problems we have been discussing. We are being forced to change, to look at more effective ways to do missions. That is a blessing. And, this is also the perspective of missions-aware laymen and women in the pew.
>   —Layperson on the board of several agencies

Interpreting the Meaning Behind the Words

At the risk of oversimplifying all that was heard in the ten sessions, the following synthesis highlights the priority issues.

1. Categorically, the single strongest commonality was that the local church is retaking the initiative for mission. Any relationship with sending agencies should be one of equals and partners. The issue of control is a major sticking point.

2. The church in the world, especially in the Southern and Eastern blocs, is much more dynamic than the troubled churches in the West. Has God moved the flame of God's presence out of the North?

3. A passion for mission is on the wane, compared with ten years ago. Pastors are torn by many agendas. There is a compassion depletion.

4. There is less concern with geography. The world has come to us. Even inner city black ministries are having to focus on immigrants. We have moved from geographic to functional interests in both church and mission.

5. The younger generation is not committed to long-term or career mission. Involvement is the watchword, and especially with their own generation.

6. Below the surface is a lot of anger. It is as if churches are saying, "We can't keep up." A big question is, can we focus on the task without needing an enemy, a demon, or an evil empire as a whipping boy?

7. Short-termers drive the vision. Involvement breaks the guilt block because they get more than they give. The approach too often is not linked to long-term strategies.

8. We must recover a sense of place for the church—a recovery of community and parish. This includes a theology related to the poor, who are not a part of suburban evangelical reality.

9. The current outlook is business as usual. Financial pressures bring us back to hard choices and forced priorities.

10. Without renewal the system is not sustainable. Big money goes into buildings. God may not be the center of worship, yet this kind of church seems to be determining the shape of twenty-first century mission in the U.S.

Part Three

How Shall They Be Sent?

How shall they be sent? There are those within churches who no longer ask that question. Some ask, "Why should they be sent?" Sadder still, some no longer ask any questions. The swirling winds of change mentioned in the introduction to this book have the strength to set in motion the "numbing down" of the church. Global realities have influenced the emerging shapes of churchly realities. The testimony of those involved in the Taskforce: 21st Century Missions project yields ample evidence of the impact of the world on the church. When we reduce the mission of God to a program or a project, only the passionate pay attention, and even then the passion may be misdirected. To ignore the problem is to invite disaster.

GLITCH IN MISSIONS EDUCATION

It has been called the Millennium Bug, that mainframe computer programming glitch that involves a shorthand piece of computer code which allows the 19 on all dates to be automatically filled in by the computer. That's all well and good and cost-saving … until December 31, 1999, when one final tick of the clock will send most computers back to 1900.

Think of the enormous work hours that will be concentrated on "undoing" the glitch. The Social Security Administration estimates it will take 300 person-years to make the changes in its system. Emil Vajda says in a recent issue of *Working Woman*, "It's all grunt work. And in the end, you have nothing to show for it. If you succeed in fixing it, you wind up with the same system that worked before. You haven't provided any new functionality; you haven't done anything that will get you promoted. But if you slip up and miss something, on January 1, 2000, your system goes down and so does your job." No more than 3 percent of all businesses have made the necessary changes.

Ralph Winter said it. Larry Walker at ACMC (Advancing Churches in Missions Commitment) says it. Missions mobilizers Bob Sjogren, and Bill and Amy Stearns say it. And now focus group leaders from churches and mission agencies across the U.S. have said it, too: There is a glitch in the missions education system.

We have been using a shorthand that assumed everyone else was filling in a critical element in the mission enterprise. Now the clock is ticking and change is demanded. Effective missions education is desperately needed.

We see it in black and white in the *Mission Mobilizers Handbook*:

> The number one priority is more mission mobilizers—mission pastors, more active mission committees, more missionary education on the local level.

"Why do I say this?" Ralph Winter asks, and says, "Because I believe there must be at least 40,000 younger adults who have in the past few years made a missionary decision but who will never make it to the field—due to local ignorance, indifference, baby-boomer detachment, school debts, etc. Only crash education can stem the downward spiral. Anyone who can help 100 missionaries to the field is more important than one missionary on the field."

In a recent consultation of mission agencies, publishers and mobilizers, Bill Stearns commented, "There are two problems in the efforts to accomplish the missions task: one, churches are frantic for missions education, and two, who cares?" For many who long for the church to understand and be radically involved in the mission of God, it would appear that no one cares enough to provide effective, ongoing opportunities for missions awareness and involvement in the church.

Larry Walker, southwest representative for ACMC, notes four obstacles to advancing churches in missions:

- ❖ A common perception that mission is peripheral to Christianity;
- ❖ The ineffectiveness of mission leaders and enthusiasts in relating missions to contemporary audiences;
- ❖ The nature of pastoral ministry which tends to focus on local needs; and
- ❖ The influence of North American culture on the evangelical church.

Walker says, "The methods and techniques that fueled the tremendous post-World War II missions mobilization effort are ineffective when used with contemporary audiences. If the North American mission industry is to continue to play a key role in reaching the unreached, we must change or die" ("Seven Dynamics for Advancing Your Church in Missions" in *Mission Mobilizers Handbook)*!

Educate to Mobilize, or Mobilize to Educate?

In *Run With the Vision*, authors Sjogren and Stearns speak of four dynamics for an integrated overall mission of the church:

- ❖ God blesses his people to strengthen the church;
- ❖ The church is to bless every people group—including its own in evangelism, ministering to community needs, and in standing up for righteousness in one's own people group;
- ❖ The church is to bless every people group, including reached peoples; and
- ❖ The church is to bless every people group, including the remaining unreached peoples of the world.

The authors say, "An integrated vision in a fellowship is not only specific. It is also non-competitive. . . . Folks whose interests and ministries concentrate on . . . seeing an unreached people discipled nevertheless affirm the other God-given ministries of the fellowship. These mission fanatics know that frontier mission efforts desperately need a strong power base. So the true mission visionary thinks through how the various home-front ministries fit into the overall mission of the church." Sjogren and Stearns feel that good missions people encourage and promote various activities that, on the surface, do not seem to relate to missions, such as the women's aerobics group, a new building program, a second grade boys' Sunday school class and fishing trip—and many others that do not seem to focus directly on unreached people.

Diverse ministries in the local church, like those listed above, might appear to fit Walker's list of obstacles to a church's advance in missions. They escape such a charge if they are part of an integrated and noncompetitive strategy for the whole church to proclaim the whole gospel in the whole world.

Whether you call it missions education or missions mobilization, the crossroads in which the missions community finds itself demands such a prioritized and integrated strategic element. Suffering from the malaise that often accompanies an assignment that is "everyone's responsibility," missions education has been no one's priority. In many situations, it has become only

❖ A returning missionary's slide show and curio table at the annual missions conference;

❖ The lone bulletin board with photos of missionaries connected by yarn to the field and the church "at home";

❖ A few weeks of preparation before a short-term mission trip;

❖ The youth missions trip;

❖ A program or kid's club option to keep the children busy; and

❖ An annual emphasis to raise missions funds.

Like the labor-intensive efforts to cure the Millennium Bug, much of the missions education effort has become laborious and mundane. In the end, the mission enterprise has nothing to show for it, providing no new functionality, no promotion of what God is doing around the world.

I am not criticizing the slide show, mission conference, bulletin board, mission trip, kid's club, offering emphasis or administrative or missions committee. Some of these projects and activities may indeed be used as tools to create a missions learning environment. But to consider that any one of these activities can accomplish the task alone is hazardous. Many of our churches face dangerous situations related to missions education as they flounder in what to do after the big missions conference or when the team returns home from a short-term project.

In reality, there are many churches that are actively pursuing a holistic approach to missions education. They combine a number of projects and activities, doing them with both the field and the congregation's needs in mind, and creating exciting models toward a missions sensitive learning environment. There are notable examples of how churches are determining their role in God's global plan.

- ❖ Presenting the biblical foundation from Genesis to Revelation, then moving from the biblical to the historical, cultural and strategic perspectives of missions.
- ❖ Setting the stage for goers, senders, welcomers and mobilizers to respond.
- ❖ Applying conceptual approaches that allow children and adults to understand God's missionary purpose and how they can play a part.
- ❖ Offering age-level appropriate organizations that address specific learning styles and learner needs.
- ❖ Providing a churchwide approach of awareness through one-time events, short-term projects and ongoing ministries.

What differs from the two lists are the intentionality of the holistic viewpoint (strategy), an awareness of audience needs and the resources to meet those needs, and the understanding that missions education is integral to the church's educational environment. To present it another way is an understanding of the implied question waiting to be asked in Romans 10:14-15 (NRSV):

> *But how are they to call on one in whom they have not believed? And how are they to believe in one of whom they have never heard? And how are they to hear without someone to proclaim him? And how are they to proclaim him unless they are sent?*

The question is, How can they be sent if no one knows to do it?

Creating that transforming awareness is what missions mobilizers focus on in ever- increasing numbers. Where are the mobilizers? Some, like Ellen Livingood of TEAM, David Dougherty of OMF, Scott Harris of SIM, Don Apgar of Wycliffe, Marjorie Hamilton of Arab World Ministries and consultant James Engel of Eastern College, can be found working together to research what types of innovative responses are needed and how their agencies can cooperate in new ways to provide those responses. Some are leading mobilizing entities like those listed in Appendix A.

Some are Perspectives course coordinators who have provided a life-changing experience for more than 30,000 who have heard the "big picture" of Bible, history, culture and strategy through the 15-week missions course. Some, like Bob Sjogren and Jill Harris of Destinations 2000 and Bill and Amy Stearns of World Christian, are consulting with churches on customized applications after making big picture presentations of the biblical foundation for God's heart for the nations.

There are communication links on the Internet like Brigada Network, which passed the 5,000 mark in participants just prior to its second birthday and includes more than 70 e-mail activated conferences on missions-related topics, prayer and unreached peoples.

KidsCan Network, founded by Jan Bell, offers ten "P" words as a framework for providing children a biblical worldview with which to interpret Scripture, missionary stories and current events. (The ten "P" words are: God's purpose and power, people, people-moving, passport to the world, possessions, projects, preparation, partnership, proclamation.) There are events such as Mission Fests, Adopt-a-People partnerships, Praying through the Window campaigns, prayer walks, and a new and growing interest in children's missions education.

In the midst of so many energized activities, there are denominationally-linked organizations that have shown themselves open to God-directed opportunities. Many, like Woman's Missionary Union (WMU), are asking, What more could or should be done?

While very effective in mobilizing Southern Baptists for missions for over 100 years, the materials that WMU produced were directed exclusively to the denomination's mission boards and missionaries, making their use inapplicable to other groups.

Today, however, WMU's vision statement is broad and inclusive, and calls for uniting efforts in more effective mobilization:

> WMU challenges Christian believers to understand and be radically involved in the mission of God.

Lyle Schaller, an authority on church growth and planning, says WMU's uniqueness has come from the ability to raise the commitment level of its members by modeling what a focus on missions is all about. WMU has sought to glorify God with such efforts as:

- ❖ Daily focused prayer for missionaries and unreached peoples;
- ❖ Lifelong learning through 15 magazines and more than 70 publications annually;
- ❖ Diverse ministries that start locally and extend globally;
- ❖ Programs in the forms of age-level organizations which now include more than one million members from preschoolers to adults, and which provide a nurturing atmosphere from which numerous missionaries first felt God's call on their lives; and
- ❖ Promoting the gathering of more than $2 billion in missions offerings throughout its 109-year history.

According to Schaller, the following represent not only the biggest challenges to pastors today but can also serve as a list of what effective missions mobilizers do best:

- ❖ Raise commitment level of congregations;

❖ Enlarge the number of volunteers;

❖ Enlarge the number of trained and skilled volunteers;

❖ Expand the teaching ministry;

❖ Raise the level of giving;

❖ Strengthen emphasis on missions; and

❖ Bring in more people (provide more attractive entry points into the church).

PAVE A PATH TO THE FUTURE

In seeking ways to equip and involve our churches in missions, we must first focus on new realities as we are propelled or pulled into the next century. In another time, churches could rely on the "if the doors are open, I'll be there" mentality of church attendance and participation. We could assume a certain level of biblical awareness on the part of church members because attendance at Sunday school was a given.

Those days are gone. Church attendance is sporadic, often based on the activity that best meets "my needs." We cannot assume a familiarity with the Scriptures adequate to provide a firm basis for understanding God's heart for the world. Mission education must be saturated with the biblical revelation of the mission of God, the model of Christ and the mandate to the church to be the proclaiming servants of God's good news.

Second, the current smorgasbord mindset in Christian education provides a formidable challenge. As we look at limited time slots available in church schedules, we must explore what more we can do with church-wide emphases, and integrate missions throughout the life of the church.

Finally, as all organizations are looking more closely at generational distinctives, we must pay more attention to the unnamed fourteenth generation and its impact on the missions scene. Recall comments from the Taskforce: 21st Century Missions project when Buster Generation missions leaders made very clear the distinctives between them and the older generation. Research becomes a driving force for the future with the implication that we will then provide the resources to meet the needs we find. From the quality demands of the Boomers to the hands-on involvement focus of the Busters, there are mounting pressures to move from what has been a print focus to more multimedia teaching and application tools.

In an ideal scenario, missions education becomes synonymous with Christian education. The church embraces its role in bringing all the nations to the worship of God by creating an environment out of which people minister, go, send, welcome those from other cultures, and mobilize for further involvement. Every church possesses an environment that stresses learning about missions, praying and giving to missions, doing missions locally and going as a volunteer or a career missionary. The totality of the Scripture, from Genesis to Revelation, will not only be revealed but also understood and assumed as the motivation behind all mission endeavors.

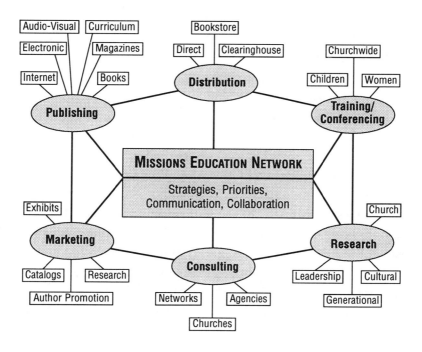

Figure 3.1. Mission extension network.

And we'll do it all with Star Trek uniforms and tractor beams at our disposal!

Well, maybe not quite. But the vision painted above is possible. While we may not achieve perfection in these earthly forms, we can pursue God's heart. From the Abrahamic covenant to the throne in Revelation, it is clear that God wants to be worshipped by all, served by all, to redeem all. While we may not reach every single individual, we can reach all unreached people groups. While we may not touch every human need, we can touch the needy within reach.

If missions education becomes more than just the cheer of passionate but peripheral players, and instead finds itself among the church priorities, and if that person of passion has access to user-friendly, culturally sensitive, age-level appropriate educational tools, missions education can permeate the church. It can encourage a partnership with God that ignites the cold critic, enlarges the tent of the narrow-minded and ultimately transforms a congregation.

So What Must We Do?

To realize this potential, an understanding of the power of the body of Christ is absolutely vital. We must work to connect, to network, to lay aside histories and semantic barriers and find a place for alliances that build on strengths, shore up weaknesses and avoid needless redundancies.

We must address publishing concerns and priorities, finding the most effective vehicle and "driver" for that vehicle to reach the intended audience.

We must study marketing and distribution. For instance, children's workers with a heart for how God can use children in prayer and ministry have cried out for a type of clearinghouse that will research diverse materials, determine strengths and weaknesses, and make recommendations from a user's standpoint. They want easy access to materials and a timely way to know what is available. Peter Hohmann, founder of Bridge Builders, writes in *Children in Crisis* (MARC, 1996), "Children's programs have often emphasized three things: sitting still, being quiet, and listening. Should we be surprised when, as adults, they continue to do what they have been taught? By the time children reach adulthood, almost all their attitudes are formed. Why not form in the child the attitude that direct involvement in God's purpose is the norm?"

To do so will mean recognizing that volunteer leaders in the church do not automatically burst onto the scene with all knowledge of learning styles and appropriate activities. Training teachers is a priority request of several mission mobilizers. The International Children's Expo offered by Jill Harris of Destinations 2000 is a welcome response, but one limited to geography and time. KidsCan e-mail network provides for idea exchange. ACMC provides workshops at its conferences. WMU provides attention to various learning styles for magazines of age-level organizations. But what about a comprehensive training plan that follows a strategy developed by these and other concerned mobilizers?

Consulting with churches about the best materials and approaches to mobilize their members requires gifted "translators" who can see a need, draw on a vast amount of stored knowledge and introduce appropriately a response customized for that individual situation. Keeping a consulting force trained and updated on available resources and current educational methodologies is a time-consuming endeavor. Can a cooperative training plan be devised whereby church relations personnel from all mission agencies may meet and share their experience annually?

Research is important. As we look at unreached peoples we easily agree that research into the culture helps opens doors. The North American church culture is in constant change. Continuing combined research efforts with shared results would enhance mission education by incredible degrees.

Recently Time and TV Guide devoted their cover stories to the subject of God. Readers of TV Guide were treated to a wide spectrum of thought from some of their favorites.

> Cures don't always come. What we settled on was that the miracle is not in the cure but in finding the strength to accept what has happened.
> —Producer-Writer Carol Binder, "Dr. Quinn, Medicine Woman"

> I think faith informs almost every episode. I'm a skeptic who desperately wants some reason to believe.
>
> —Chris Carter, "The X-Files" Creator

> If we are being as brazen as to invoke the name of God on TV, if we're doing it poorly, I just don't think God would bless the show and allow it to continue.
>
> —Angel of death actor John Dye, "Touched by an Angel"

The above statements reveal a search for spirituality supported by the magazine's poll of 804 adults. Sixty-one percent of the respondents said they would like to see more references to God, churchgoing and other religious observance in prime time, and 68% said they were particularly eager to see more prime time spirituality.

The magazine chose to define "spirituality" as a "belief in a higher being, but not necessarily an affiliation with a particular organized religion," a path of least resistance when working within the mindset that "religion is not an easy subject to handle. It reaches deep into our sense of self, and there are as many different experiences of faith as there are people in the world."

The question for the missions community is whether or not it can simply continue to acknowledge the impact of secular media on our culture or, with our educator-translator roles intact, can begin to use the media as a tool in education. Perhaps we could even influence what finds its way onto the screen.

We are faced with the potential of a comprehensive view of missions education that stops not at the door of a classroom, not at the cover of a curriculum piece, not at the home page of a Web site, but moves to one of the recognized shapers of current thinking. Rather than merely lamenting the power of media to shift attention to hot spots, can we create a strategy for education that includes a media effort to answer the skeptics who want some reason to believe?

The parallels are not exact, but in many ways the translator analogy will again serve us well. Like the translator, mission educators need to know their source, the entity for which they will be translating. Do mission mobilizers have easy access to mission agencies? Like the translator, mission educators need to know the audience to whom they are translating. Are we doing the research needed to understand the culture of the North American church and its leaders? If so, are we sharing what we know and insuring that we avoid redundant efforts? Like the translator, the mission educator must know the language and all available options to translate not just the words but also the concepts and context of the message. Are we keeping up with technology, with educational advances, with learning styles and methodologies?

In a recent presentation to those interested in development issues, the speaker noted that there are two kinds of economists: those who don't know the future and those who don't know that they don't know. Mission specialists in the focus groups that met across America all knew that there was a glitch in the mission education system and that something needed to be done about it in the pew, the pulpit and in theological training centers. But there was great confusion as to whose responsibility it was: The mission agency? The seminary? The church? Publishers? Specialized mission education entities? Yes to all of the above, to some degree. But we now know in a twenty-first century world we need a balanced, comprehensive, sequential, audience-appropriate approach. Collaborative networks and alliances are the future for mission education in the next millennium. This just may be the solution that will move us from merely fixing a problem to paving a path beyond this current crossroads and into exciting directions empowered by God's heart for the nations.

Part Four

Getting Inside the Future

TIME AND THE TIMES

Now abide the past, the present, and the future—these three. But the greatest of these is . . . ? What a question to ask the church! To answer it assumes it is a valid question. But what kind of question is it really? An eschatological question, or a modernity question firmly rooted in an Enlightenment linear thinking mentality? How the U.S. mission community deals with that question may determine whether its role in a global mission endeavor during the twenty-first century will even be appropriate, much less effective. In short, the church must deal with an understanding of time, and the times.

David Bosch quotes Ernst Troeltsch, who said of twentieth century theology, "The eschatology office is mostly closed." Many conceded that we were living in a closed universe where purpose gave way to the pragmatic. We digitalized and segmented chronology into insulated capsules of past/present/future. We redefined God's right moment, *kairos*, as chance, luck or just happening to be in the right place at the right time. During that era one segment of the church took its agenda from the world, often saying the modern missions movement was over. Another segment prided itself on "being faithful to the Word of God" while reducing mission to programs and projects, describing success in pragmatic cause-effect terms. Acculturation is no respecter of positions on a theological spectrum. Meanwhile, the younger Now Generation jettisoned the past, denied a future and collapsed all existence into the black hole of a meaningless now.

Bosch also posted notice that in the last half of the twentieth century the door to the eschatology office has cracked open again. It is a reminder that Jesus' response to the Pharisees and Sadducees who asked him to show them a sign from heaven is still valid today. Acknowledging that they were adept at interpreting the appearance of the sky as it pertained to weather (equivalent of monitoring trends?), the only sign that would be given was the sign of Jonah. Jesus broke into the eyes of the public with the announcement that the kingdom was near, requiring a repenting, turnaround experience.

The Cross-Resurrection event within Creation's timeframe compressed notions of a past and future into the eternal present-ness of the great I Am. Within that timeless frame we can escape from a definition of past as mere recall and future as foggy anticipation. We also live in a *now*. But, rather than a black hole of meaninglessness, the God of Purpose inhabits this now. In this now we embrace and understand the correlation between visions of creation and visions of the end. This now is full of the past and the future. Its liturgy consists of memory and hope. Its modus operandi is love.

As Christ-followers it is crucial that we understand time and the times from within that framework, and know what to do about it, not unlike the leaders from the tribe of Issachar during the days young David was on the run. From eleven of the tribes of Israel more than 300,000 men who were ready for battle defected from Saul to David. But from one tribe, Issachar, only 200 were reported. And these were not armed with weapons. Rather, the reporter described them as those who "understood the times, and knew what to do."

How desperately we need ministers of foresight in our own time! It will require meeting regularly at the Eucharistic table, keeping alive the memory that fuels our story. It is equally important that we engage in the

Easter dance in front of an empty tomb. The reality behind and beyond its emptiness is the basis of hope that also fuels our story. It is in this kind of worship that our story is kept alive. Therein we maintain both our identity and our reason for being. We remember that God as Tri-unity (Trinity) with diverse dimensions created a com-unity (community) with diverse gifts. The community is the visible link between God, people and nature. In our pilgrimage together the community looks like and acts like God, being both just and merciful.

Although we live in a world out of sync and out of relationship with the God of purpose, it is still possible to be good hands and feet to carry out the will of the Head as our love continuously focuses on God and neighbor simultaneously. And, it is possible to know who and where our neighbor is. Our neighbors are in all those places prepared for us. Since Christ is already there, we are to be there too, with Christ and neighbor simultaneously. That is the ideal. It should be the norm. And we have a God-given borderless timescape in which to live out that norm.

The problem arises because the rhythm of God's mission (*missio Dei*) is counter to that of time-bound orchestrations. Either the cacophonies of cultural dissonance drown out our own story on the one hand, or in some strange way lure us into joining in the world's song on the other. If we are not careful we lose the feel for our story, and may even forget it. What will be the fate of missions in the twenty-first century if the community is forgetful, fragmented and faithless? Only a kind of worship that fuels memory and hope can sustain the church on its pilgrimage and provide a place for us in that borderless timescape from which we can chart our involvement in God's mission.

Memory

Let's imagine we are sitting at the table of Communion. The Word of God, living and written, comes alive in the act of remembering.

❖ Abram, you will become a blessing to all the ethnic peoples of the world.

❖ What does God require of you but to do justice, love mercy, and walk humbly with your God?

❖ Love the Lord your God with all your heart, mind, soul. And don't forget, love your neighbor as yourself. *All* the law and the prophets hang on these two commandments.

❖ The Spirit of the Lord is upon me because he has anointed me to preach good news to the poor. He has sent me to proclaim freedom for the prisoners and recovery of sight for the blind, to release the oppressed, to proclaim the year of the Lord's favor.

❖ I am going there to prepare a place for you ... I will come back and take you to be with me that you may also be where I am.

❖ As the Father sent me, so I am sending you.

Hope

Since faith is a backward look that fuels our courage to turn around and take the next pilgrim steps, how can we get a clear vision of where God is taking us, and how can we apply it?

First, we must keep alive the story that shapes us. The story embodies our hope.

❖ God loves everyone and has purpose for all.

❖ God wants everyone to know that.

❖ God creates community in which everyone can know God's love and purpose.

❖ The community has fragmented, lost its way. Fallen, self-centered humanity cannot, on its own, achieve personal or communal wholeness.

❖ God's love and purpose for everyone, and all creation, initiates the way by which right relationships can be restored, with God and with our neighbors.

Already and Not Yet

Already—not yet. The reign of God has already broken into human history but is not yet complete. The church on pilgrimage is to be a colony of heaven on earth, living out the future as if it were already present. This colony that embraces memory and hope is designed to live out of its future, with full faith in the God who created it for God's own missional purposes. The problem lies in that we have been planted in a hostile culture, complicated and convulsed by rapid and volatile changes. Many think we are living through the birth pains of a new civilization.

What is the new civilization like? For one thing, new notions and alignments of human endeavor already accompany accelerating global change. Personal freedom, economic empowerment, advanced technological capabilities, new problems and new perspectives on humankind will increasingly disrupt traditional, even ancient expectations and patterns.

While Toffler describes a *trisected* world in terms of civilizations, Robert Schreiter in *The New Catholicity: Theology Between the Global and the Local*, describes the world moving politically to *multipolar* realities after the demise of the ideology of the Second World. Although no one has mapped this new configuration persuasively, Schreiter describes the "decrease in the importance of territory or contiguity as a way of mapping reality."

Economically, Schreiter talks about a *single world*. He points out that with the demise of Second World state socialism as an economic possibility we are seeing the expansion of worldwide market capitalism: "It is characterized by its ignoring of national boundaries, its ability to move capital quickly, and its engagement in short-term projects that maximize the profit margin."

Consider the seeming contradiction of numbers in the above characteristics: single, triple, multiple. To further complicate the matter Schreiter discusses globalization as compression. "Technological innovations compress both our sense of time and our sense of space. . . . The rapidity of movement disparages attaching any significance to the past and makes the future ever more short-term. Time becomes a present with an edge of future, reminding us of the constant obsolescence of the past. Our sense of space is also compressed, symbolized in the computer chip."

With the blurring of boundaries between states, and the inability of governments to control the flow of information and money across these outdated lines, a whole new dynamic has been set up. Schreiter states it succinctly: "If boundaries play an important role in the semiotics of identity by helping us define who we are by who we are not, they are now so crisscrossed by globalization processes that they seem to have lost their identity-conferring power." Add to all this an increasingly homogenized world culturally vis-a-vis the penetration of Western culture to the corners of the earth, a differentiated world ethnically as tribes seek to conserve their identity, and a pluralistic world religiously. People are losing their sense of identity.

If the church mission is to be a robust enterprise in the twenty-first century, new ways of approaching the future and using our vision must be found. New concepts and capabilities must be imagined. "One of the greatest assets we have is that virtually all definitions are up for re-defining, and paradigms for re-paradigming," says NASA scientist John Anderson. The situation should be viewed as unprecedented opportunity. What is needed is a mechanism for carrying out such a fundamental exercise that moves us beyond feeling our way into a dimly lit future while continuing business as usual.

Christ-followers should not be alarmed by the prospect of massive change. God has already given us a way to get into the future and see the end from the beginning. With the emergence of Third Wave civilization, the so-called Information Era moved right onto the church's turf. Christ came proclaiming that the reign of God was now present. As French missioner Lucien Legrand reminds us in Unity and Plurality, "Before saying the words of God, Jesus was the very Word of God." Jesus empowered others to be proclaimers and informers of the same Good News he came bearing. Legrand states that it was a deed that was announced, not a doctrine: "A deed is proclaimed. A doctrine is taught."

The first Christ-followers did not merely announce their speculations. They boldly proclaimed a deed that was so all-encompassing it reached out to include the future in the body of the announcement.

Those proclaimers were not clairvoyant. They experienced the Christ on the other side of his death. From a future framework they set in motion a legacy for the church in every age: Inform, announce, proclaim the good news about the fact of God, and God's love for all persons, all creation. At its best the church can say that it has been over into the future and it works. There need be no contradiction in combining spiritual discernment with processes aimed at building missional pathways for the pilgrimage into the unknown.

A new and very effective process for seeing and thinking out of the future was developed by John Anderson while serving as director of the Advanced Concepts Division of NASA.

HORIZON MISSION METHODOLOGY

John Anderson of NASA developed a methodology for achieving breakthroughs in space technology, devising new ways of approaching the future. Anderson knew that if all NASA could do in its space missions was to enhance the last breakthrough, making it bigger or better for the next experiment, the space program would be dead in the water.

Horizon Mission Methodology is a highly structured five-step process for thinking outside the "flashlight beam" as we peer into the future. Anderson knew that in looking toward the future, humans typically extrapolate or project from present knowledge. He states, "We metaphorically shine 'flashlight beams' from the present into the future onto a dark wall (see Figure 4.1)." But the only future we see by doing this is the portion of the wall illuminated by a beam. What we see is what our paradigms let us see. But disturbingly, we know that much of the future lies outside those beams."

Anderson's own description of the process steps follows:

Step 1 - Leap (Leap outside the flashlight beam)

This is an intuitive leap outside the "flashlight beam" to create an extraordinary, "impossible," mind-blowing future beyond our reach. It should be strategically relevant and plausible, but it must leapfrog foreseeable capabilities, beyond extrapolation. The Horizon must cause peo-

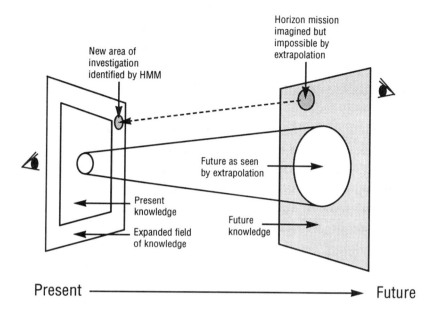

New area of
investigation
identified by HMM

Horizon mission
imagined but
impossible by
extrapolation

Future as seen
by extrapolation

Present
knowledge

Future
knowledge

Expanded field
of knowledge

Present ——————————————————→ Future

Figure 4.1. "Back from the future" flashlight beams.

ple to think in different categories, even disorient them, not just demand
more performance in familiar categories.

Step 2 - Construct (Shape a new frame of reference)

The new frame of reference is constructed by postulating radical
new properties of that Horizon as if it were a reality. Such a reality could
include critical functions, extreme performance levels, unprecedented
capabilities and novel influencing forces.

Step 3 - Think (Think within a new frame of reference)

Thinking must now take place within the new frame of reference as
if the Horizon were a reality, to identify breakthrough-based alternatives
that could have accomplished that future. This is the perspective of: I'm
here in the future. How did I get here? This is emphatically not the same
perspective as, How could I get there from here, which is the traditional
and instinctive way to address the problem. This step is difficult and

requires considerable discipline to stay on track, to think at a higher functional level than the technology answer. Stating solutions at a higher functional level is analogous to answering the question, What business are we really in?

Step 4 - Identify (Identify higher-order approaches and high-leverage capabilities)

This begins the return "back from the future" to the present frame of reference. Higher-level functions are grouped into vision-inspiring categories. Evocative metaphors are extremely productive. They help to gather, integrate and structure ideas and solutions into new categories of capability. Then the high-leverage directions are identified—those that could have the greatest impact on the future.

Step 5 - Return (Return to present frame of reference)

Back in the present, transform the high-leverage concepts by identifying near-term steps and issues. These include critical enabling technologies, drivers or motivating forces, other applications, strategic and programmatic themes. Discover new higher-level functional and cross-impact insights.

In other words, the return to the present involves some clear steps: 1) Crystallize the thinking from the earlier steps; 2) give priority status to the most plausible and relevant ideas; and 3) "backcast" them into the present. From this new present arena, turn around and walk back into the future on the steppingstones that the whole process put in place.

THE METHODOLOGY APPLIED

Anderson agreed to lead a workshop for Christian mission leaders at the Global Center of Samford University's Beeson Divinity School, engaging participants in the principles of Horizon Mission Methodology.

In introducing the workshop, Anderson stated:

> One of the most intriguing challenges in any field is to step beyond current problems and plans, issues and approaches, capabilities and technologies, to expand our concepts of the future. This is a surprisingly hard endeavor. On the one hand our culture abounds with

visions of the future drawn from studies, films, science fiction, the purposes of leaders and their pioneering enterprises. And many of the future's breakthroughs in capabilities, markets, movements, and missions already exist. But today they appear in progenitor form, almost in disguise. While these visions spark exciting possibilities, they are their own obstacles. They fall outside current paradigms, those mental or emotional "inner models of reality" that tend to govern our cognitive skills and behavior. Our paradigms act as old and aging frames of reference that seem to filter information, organize knowledge, and evaluate new ideas for us largely without our realizing it. It has been said we look for "blessings not in disguise." Our thinking becomes so caught up in our paradigms, in being incremental, or just reactive, that it misses being proactive and the prelude to inspiring visions.

If our future is to be robust, if the great human issues of our time are to be credibly addressed, new concepts and capabilities must be imagined and developed. New ways of approaching the future must be devised.

It was those "new ways" we chose to apply in the workshop with a highly diverse group of participants. (See Appendix B for a detailed description of the Horizon Mission Methodology Workshop.)

Purpose

The purpose of this ground-breaking workshop was twofold:

❖ Explore a greatly expanded concept of the global frontier and human endeavor in support of the global mission of the church;
❖ Conceptualize human relational concepts which could:
 • Enable entirely new individual and/or organizational functions and capabilities;
 • Provide quantum change in behavior and effectiveness;
 • Challenge human ingenuity; and
 • Inspire sustained support, development and expansion of the global mission of the church.

Horizon: The African Miracle

The horizon chosen for the workshop was: "The African Miracle: Emergence of a Global Power."

It is the year 2050. Africa has emerged as a global power. Independent cooperative states throughout Africa have engineered an economic, humanitarian and human rights miracle. Education, health and business are stunning successes. With inspired vision and leadership, independent African states have united.

At least three things were instrumental in this miracle: 1) An unprecedented collaboration between the church, universities, institutions and businesses; 2) the opportunity to identify, nurture and support the gifted Africans in their founding of the future Africa; and 3) communications technology—accessible to virtually every person (certainly village). This provides links to the African spirit to inspire hope and infuse knowledge.

Scope

We first leapfrogged beyond the current overwhelming problems of Africa and assumed they have been solved. Then we came "back from the future" to address those problems. The workshop was exploratory, not deterministic, so it did not conduct a complete definition of all elements, problems or requirements.

Objectives

1) Conceptualize future enterprises, capabilities, activities, technologies requiring or providing extreme performance by combinations of humans and organizations.
2) Identify critical human relational concepts that would enable these endeavors.
3) Identify high leverage relational concepts, ecclesial components and enabling mechanisms.

Developmental Themes

1) What could empower the African individual?
2) What motivational forces could attract humans to contribute to an African miracle?

3) What institutional forces would cause dramatic change?

CONCLUSIONS

The content related to the "African Miracle" was mind-stretching. But, as stated earlier, the intent was not to solve Africa's problems. Rather, we struggled with a new methodology that could help us get out of the box that may have served earlier visions of U.S. missions, but that is now suffering from conceptual cataracts.

No one can predict or forecast the future with any degree of predictability or credibility. But we can engage in visioning, which combines foresight and backcasting. By postulating a strategically relevant and plausible future, we can engage human intuition in ways that have not been available.

How does one feed the mind and soul so that the intuitive process has something from which to work? Someone has said that intuition is the distillation of experience. It will be a crippled intuition if the experience does not include a full range of mind-soul-body activities. For instance, there must be the combination of living in the real world and in the Word of God simultaneously. Those who will make a difference in twenty-first century mission activity will commit themselves continually to the kind of reading, dialogue, probing, questioning, thinking, feeling experiences that feed the mind and the heart. Journals like *The Futurist* and *Futures Research Quarterly* provide insights into the thinking of professional futurists as well as news of developments in many disciplines. Science fiction reveals the ability of those who imagine and create outside the flashlight beam, and become the inspirers of heightened imagination in others.

While the secret closet of personal reflection is one dimension of the life of a world changer, it needs the complementary dimension of interaction with a larger group. It is from sharing insights with the group that we gain instruction, correction and affirmation. Some now say we are living in the communications age. But Tony Stevenson and June Lennie describe another scenario called the "communicative age." The difference "conveys the notion that women and men are actively involved in listening to one another, sharing and negotiating meanings through conversation and cooperative activities, not merely exchanging and processing information—talking with each other not talking to each other" ("Emerging Designs for Word, Living, and Learning in the Communicative Age," *Futures Research Quarterly*, Fall 1995).

What if we could overcome the disconnectedness between the members of the U.S. missions community? What if we could let go of a sense of holy turf? What we are seeking is a virtual target common to the individual futures of missions community (see Figure 4.2).

This frontier of collaboration, which marks the last frontier in the missions effort, brings together the combined but diverse gifts of the community of faith. We listen to each other. We process information

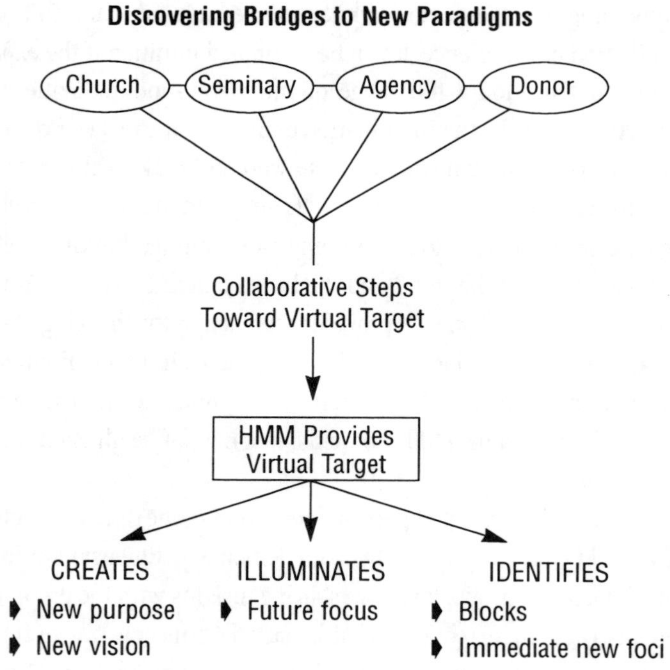

Discovering Bridges to New Paradigms

Figure 4.2. Seeking a common virtual target.

together. We share and negotiate meanings through cooperative activities. Together we go into a future framework to think critically and pray relevantly.

From the future we backcast into our present arenas, then turn around and walk together into that future. In common cause under common Lordship, we bear witness to the person and purpose of the triune God. God is glorified. And, wonder of wonders, the unbelieving world sees the unity of the body—unity achieved, not as a goal to be gained, but as a byproduct of an obedience to be demonstrated.

Epilogue

In addition to James Engel's *A Clouded Future? Advancing North American World Missions,* every pastor and mission administrator should take seriously the work of Ronald Vallet and Charles Zach, *The Mainline Church's Funding Crisis.* To quote Vincent Alfano and L.E. Siverns in one of the two forewords, "The church in North America sits in the midst of a mission funding crisis that is but another name for a crisis of identity and loyalty. . . . The church . . . is flying its flag at half mast, and the flag it is flying is white. Even a redoubling of effort when we have forgotten our aim is but philosopher George Santayana's definition of fanaticism: *"The danger to the church is not the wickedness of the few but, as Bonhoeffer reminded us, the weakness of the many"* [italics added]. And one of the glaring weaknesses is either forgetting or rejecting the stewarding role of the church as the designated hands and feet of the mission of God. The church is a subplot to the bigger story. If it exists for its own sake, or its own growth, it has probably already broken the first commandment.

There is a role for the U.S. missions community in the twenty-first century. That role will be no stronger than the churches comprising it. The good news is that throughout the evangelical missions community there is a near unanimous cry for the renewal of the church.

Therefore, we venture a closing suggestion. In this risky pilgrimage that may seem lonely, let us strive for:

Community

As the extension of the body of Christ, the local expressions of the church must recapture what it means to be a part of a larger covenant community. *The importance of place and purpose, i.e., parish and mission, must be held in appropriate balance.* Any renewal of the church that bypasses this biblical understanding will fall short of understanding the interconnectedness of the components as each one has local and global significance.

Listening

Churches in the West, and especially in the United States, must work on enhancing their "receivers." We have overworked our "transmitters." The arrogance reflected in one-way communication of the gospel ultimately creates a deafness to what the Spirit is saying through other parts of the body. Perhaps our local churches need to send members out for short-term assignments of listening, looking and absorbing what the Spirit of God is doing in other places, especially among the Two-Thirds World churches. They can, then, return home, report and help the churches to interpret what all this means. *We desperately need to assume a humble, learning posture.*

Unity

"Unity" is not a slogan, or an end in itself. *It is the* shalom *characteristic of the body of Christ that holds in appropriate balance wholeness with diversity.* One Lord, one mission, diversity of gifts. The current ecumenical movement is marked by an ecumenicity of spirit. Various churches, and the missional expressions of churches and believers, are discovering each other and experimenting with the offering of their corporate spiritual gifts to the sovereign Lord, as God creates a master mosaic in the service of the *missio Dei.* Therefore, the issue of unity must be dealt with on a broader scale than mere adherence to some creedal expressions based on human interpretations.

Gabriel Moran reminds us in *A Grammar of Responsibility* that the root meaning of responsibility comes from the Hebrew term meaning "to listen." First we hear the voice and the call of God. To hear, then, is to be "response-able." May our churches that comprise the U.S. missions community pray and humble ourselves, and seek God with all our hearts. To do so will strip us of an attitude of arrogance and a spirit of triumphalism.

Perhaps Kenneth Cragg has a word for us in "Our First Task":

> Our first task in approaching
> > another people
> > > another culture
> > > > another religion
>
> Is to take off our shoes
> > for the place we are
> > > approaching is holy.
>
> Else we may find ourselves
> treading on another's dream
> > more serious still,
> > we may forget . . .
> > > that God
> > > > was there before our arrival.

Works Cited

Part One

Drucker, Peter. "Seeing Things as They Really Are" in *Forbes*, March 10, 1997.

Popcorn, Faith. *The Popcorn Report*. New York: Harper Business, 1992.

Toffler, Alvin and Heidi . *War and Anti-war: Survival at the Dawn of the Twenty-first Century*. Boston and New York: Little, Brown & Co., 1993.

Part Three

Hohmann, Peter. "Children in Missions" in *Children in Crisis*. Monrovia: MARC, 1996.

Sjogren, Bob and Amy Stearns. *Run with the Vision*. Minneapolis: Bethany House, 1995.

TV Guide. March 29, 1997.

Walker, Larry. "Seven Dynamics for Advancing Your Church" in *Mission Mobilizer's Handbook*. Pasadena: William Carey Library, 1996.

Woodward, Kenneth L. "Is God Listening?" in *Newsweek*, March 31, 1997.

Part Four

Engel, James. *A Clouded Future? Advancing North American World Missions*. Milwaukee: Christian Stewardship, 1996.

Legrand, Lucien. *Unity and Plurality*. Maryknoll: Orbis Books, 1990.

Stevenson, Tony and June Lennie. "Emerging Designs for Work, Living, and Learning in the Communicative Age" in *Futures Research Quarterly*, Fall 1995.

EPILOGUE

Moran, Gabriel. *A Grammar of Responsibility*. New York: Crossroad Publishing, 1996.

Zach, Charles and Ronald Vallet. *The Mainline Church's Funding Crisis*. Grand Rapids: Eerdmans, 1995.

Bibliography

How does one feed the mind and soul so that the intuitive process has something from which to work? Someone has said that intuition is the distillation of experience. It will be a crippled intuition if the experience does not include a full range of mind-soul-body activities. For instance, there must be the combination of living in the real world and in the Word of God simultaneously. Those who will make a difference in twenty-first century missions activity will commit continually to the kind of reading, dialogue, probing, questioning, thinking, feeling experiences that feed the mind and the heart.

BOOKS

Bakke, Raymond. *A Theology as Big as the City*. Downers Grove: InterVarsity Press, 1997.

Bosch, David. *Transforming Mission*. Maryknoll: Orbis, 1991.

Costas, Orlando. *Liberating News: A Theology of Contextual Evangelization*. Grand Rapids: Eerdmans, 1989.

Easum, William. *Dancing with Dinosaurs: Ministry in a Hostile and Hurting World*. Nashville: Abingdon, 1993.

Drucker, Peter F. *Managing for the Future*. New York: Truman Talley Books/ Dutton, 1992.

Engel, James F. *A Clouded Future? Advancing North American World Missions*. Milwaukee: Christian Stewardship Association, 1996.

Handy, Charles. *The Age of Paradox*. Boston: Harvard Business School, 1994.

Knoke, William. *Bold New World*. New York and Tokyo: Kadansha International, 1996.

Kotkin, Joel. *Tribes*. New York: Random House, 1993.

Mead, Loren. *The Once and Future Church*. New York: Alban Institute, 1991.

Messer, Donald. *A Conspiracy of Goodness: Contemporary Images of Christian Mission*. Nashville: Abingdon, 1992.

Moran, Gabriel. *A Grammar of Responsibility*. New York: Crossroad Publishing, 1996.

Naisbitt, John. *Megatrends Asia*. New York: Simon & Schuster, 1996.

Phillips, James M., and Robert T. Coote, eds. *Toward the Twenty-first Century in Christian Mission*. Grand Rapids: Eerdmans Publishing Co., 1993.

Popcorn, Faith. *Clicking*. New York: Harper, 1996.

Roof, Wade Clark. *A Generation of Seekers: The Spiritual Journeys of Baby Boom Generation*. San Francisco: Harper Collins, 1993.

Schaller, Lyle. *Innovation in Ministry: Models for the 21st Century*. Nashville: Abingdon, 1994.

Sine, Tom. *Cease Fire*. Grand Rapids: Eerdmans, 1995.

Sjogren, Bob and Amy Stearns. *Run with the Vision*. Minneapolis: Bethany House Publishers, 1995.

Snyder, Howard. *Earth Currents: The Struggle for the World's Soul*. Nashville: Abingdon, 1995.

Toffler, Alvin and Heidi. *War and Anti-War: Survival at the Dawn of the 21st Century*. Boston and New York: Little, Brown & Co., 1993.

Vallet, Ronald and Charles Zach. *The Mainline Church's Funding Crisis*. Grand Rapids: Eerdmans, 1995.

JOURNALS

The Economist
Evangelical Missions Quarterly
Foreign Affairs
Futures Research Quarterly
The Futurist
International Bulletin of Missionary Research
Missiology
The Muslim World
National Catholic Reporter
Swing
Wilson Quarterly
Wired
World Press

Appendix A

Mission Mobilizers

ADVANCING CHURCHES IN MISSIONS COMMITMENT (ACMC)
115 Oakhurst Drive, Tyrone, GA 30290
Phone 770-631-9900
103623.1072@compuserve.com

A network of missions-active churches through which a church can get specific, practical assistance tailored to the church's global outreach needs. ACMC helps mobilize the congregation, build vision and help you become strategically involved in world evangelization, all at a price even the smallest church can afford. ACMC assists churches through a regional staff, mission resources, how-to handbooks, networking publications, conferences, vision seminars.

U.S. CENTER FOR WORLD MISSION
1605 Elizabeth Street, Pasadena, CA 91104
Phone 626-398-2200
Dave.Imboden@uscwm.org

Using the watchword, "A Church for Every People by the Year 2000," the Center calls mission agencies and churches to the plight of the unreached peoples through mobilization, training, strategy and services. The Mobilization Division assists the church by creating strategic communication tools, resources and programs necessary for quality participation in reaching the unreached and by making the church aware of resources and vital ministries. The Training Division includes Perspectives on the World Christian Movement, a graduate and undergraduate level introduction to mission focusing on the biblical, historical, strategic and cultural perspectives; World Christian Foundations; Serve, Work & Study program. The Strategy Division stresses three objectives: (1) to provide research on who and where unreached peoples are; (2) to discover what has been or may be successful in penetrating these peoples with the gospel; and (3) to provide training classes and seminars on the Muslim, Hindu, Buddhist, etc. worlds. The Services Division includes practical help such as technical assistance, media resources (Frontier Media) and William Carey Library.

ASSOCIATION OF INTERNATIONAL MISSION SERVICES
P.O. Box 64534, Virginia Beach, VA 23464
Phone 757-579-5850
AIMS@cbn.org
http://www.regent, edu/aims
   A ministry fellowship to awaken the global Christian community to world evangelization through praying, giving and going; encouraging and facilitating fellowship, networking and communication among Great Commission Christians; advocate strategic evangelization and targeting of unreached peoples; mobilize and train AIMS' members and partners for effective participation in front-line missions; cooperate with the great body of Christ to work toward world evangelization.

CALEB PROJECT
#10 West Dry Creek Circle
Littleton, CO 80120-4413
phone: 303-730-4170
info@cproject.com
http://www.goshen.net/cproject/
   Presentations, individual counseling, short-term field projects and media resource development and distribution that encourage and assist

baby boomers and baby busters to complete their part in evangelizing the world. Attention focused on the needs of the least-evangelized people groups in the world.

ASSOCIATION OF CHRISTIAN MINISTRIES TO INTERNATIONALS
7 Switchbud Place, C 192-209
The Woodlands, TX 77380
Phone 713-367-5020

An association of individuals who minister to internationals either as volunteers or as professionals, and of churches and parachurch ministries which focus upon outreach to internationals.

LAUSANNE COMMITTEE FOR WORLD EVANGELIZATION
Bakkegardsveien 9
1450 Nesoddtangen, Norway
Phone/fax +47 66912775
lausanne@powertech.no

The Lausanne Committee represents the third phase of a movement launched in Lausanne, Switzerland, in 1974 by the inspiration and leadership of Billy Graham. The Lausanne Covenant became the foundational expression for evangelicals across the world to engage in proclaiming the gospel to all nations. Lausanne II was held in Manila, Philippines, in 1989. The effectiveness of the movement since 1974 was marked by successful initiatives begun by agencies, groups and individuals all across the world. The current Lausanne Committee serves as a motivator and catalyst for all those engaged in world evangelization, as well as resourcing regional initiatives.

AD 2000 AND BEYOND
2960 South Circle Drive #2112
Colorado Springs, CO 80906
Phone 719-576-2000
http://www.ad2000.org/

A global evangelization movement stressing greater mutual awareness of their efforts to mobilize the worldwide body of Christ for world evangelization by A.D. 2000; encouraging, motivating and networking church leaders by inspiring them with the vision of reaching the unreached by A.D. 2000 through consultations, prayer efforts and written materials. Global networks include the Cities Resource Network, Unreached Peoples, Pastors Mobilization, Radio Task Force, Women's Track, National Research Mobilization.

MISSION AMERICA
901 East 78th Street, Minneapolis, MN 55420
Phone 612-853-1762
74152.636@compuserve.com

A mobilization network with the stated goal of mobilizing "the whole U.S. church to take the whole gospel to the whole nation in this generation: and to mobilize thousands of new cross-cultural missionaries to team with brothers and sisters from other nations of the world in going to the unreached peoples of the world, including the millions of unreached peoples residing in the 10/40 Window."

CHRISTIAN INFORMATION NETWORK
11025 State Highway 83, Colorado Springs, CO 80921.
Phone 719-522-1040
73422.3471@compuserve.com

Provides prayer information on the 10/40 Window and 100 gateway cities; facilitates the international "Praying Through the Window" campaigns.

(Information from *Mission Mobilizers Handbook*, published by William Carey Library, Pasadena, Calif., 1996)

Appendix B

Horizon Mission Methodology Workshop

John L. Anderson

A Horizon Mission Methodology (HMM) workshop was conducted for mission leaders, taking as a challenging exercise the defining of conditions that would either cause or result from the emergence of Africa as a global power in 2050.

The workshop had two purposes. One was to expose mission leaders to the use of the Horizon Mission Methodology, to see if there were transferable principles from its use in science to a new way of thinking about twenty-first century missiology. The second purpose was to describe human relational concepts that could: permit entirely new individual and/or organizational functions and capabilities; provide quantum changes in personal behavior and organizational effectiveness; challenge human ingenuity; and inspire sustained support of the global mission of the church.

It should be emphasized that the Horizon Mission Methodology process is not a planning tool, but a new way of thinking about and seeing the future. Through these heightened and expanded ways of seeing and understanding we can more effectively work in the present.

The workshop was sponsored by William R. O'Brien, director of the Global Center of the Beeson Divinity School of Samford University. It was held February 6-7, 1997, in Birmingham, Alabama. The 36 attendees represented most major Christian denominations, with participants from Zimbabwe, Liberia, Zaire, Kenya and the U.S. The workshop was conducted by John L. Anderson of NASA, developer of the Horizon Mission Methodology (HMM).

What is Horizon Mission Methodology?

In looking toward the future, humans typically extrapolate from present knowledge. We metaphorically shine "flashlight beams" from the present into the future, "onto a dark wall." The only future we see by doing this is the portion of the wall illuminated by the beam. What we see is what our paradigms let us see. But we know that much of the future lies outside those beams.

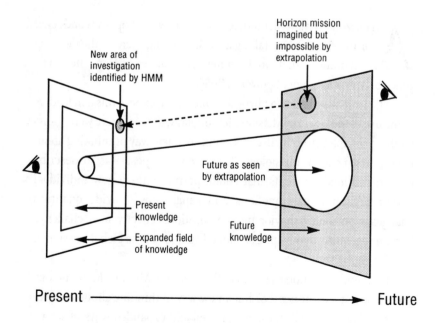

Figure 1. "Back from the future" flashlight beams.

The Horizon Mission Methodology (HMM) is a strategy for getting outside those "flashlight beams" to think more creatively (see Figure 1). It is a highly structured five-step process for first creating and then thinking within an entirely new frame of reference based on a specific hypothetical future called a Horizon Mission. Horizon "Missions" may also be "Capabilities" or "Axioms."

A "Horizon" is a truly challenging future, a leap of imagination beyond our reach. Such a horizon is never intended to be an actual goal, necessarily. It is simply an artifice that blocks linear, extrapolative thinking and forces non-linear, intuitive, leap-frog thinking. The HMM was developed for aerospace science and technology, but because it deals with basic human thought processes and our conceptual limits, it applies to any arena in which radically new perspectives and concepts are wanted.

Africa a Global Power?

The hypothetical horizon addressed in this February 1997 workshop was "The Emergence of Africa as a Global Power in 2050." We attempted to envision that from its generally abysmal state a half century ago (the year 2000), Africa by a.d. 2050 has risen like a phoenix to become a global power. Independent, cooperative states throughout Africa have achieved an institutional, economic and human rights miracle. Education, health and business are stunning successes. The global mission of the church has been an instrumental part of the inspired vision and leadership responsible for this emergence. The rationale for this choice of Horizon Mission is as follows:

- ❖ Africa has long been a subject of Christian mission.
- ❖ Strong seeds of Christianity already exist.
- ❖ Extreme poverty and disease make it a top priority for humanitarian interest.
- ❖ It has enormous resources (undeveloped wealth of minerals and natural beauty).
- ❖ Business investment and tourism offer a way to infuse massive financial resources.

❖ Africa's current weaknesses after colonialism make it more malleable for transformation (in contrast to strong Islamic states).

❖ The fact that Africa is not a monolithic state offers many points of entry to introduce a long- term African Emergence Program.

❖ States already exist that could be groomed to be anchors for actions (e.g., South Africa).

❖ The African Americans, their churches and Africans in American communities should be inspired to support this African Emergence (perhaps forming a Peace Corps equivalent).

❖ If ever there was a global problem requiring new paradigms, radical new approaches and strong innovative leadership, this is it.

It is important to understand that using a far-term Africa 2050 Global Power as a Horizon Mission does not mean it is a committed strategic intent of any organization. It is simply a mental artifice. It presents a challenge of sufficient magnitude and emotional interest that any solution concepts found for it would be easily adaptable to related challenges or other mission options.

WORKSHOP PROCESS AND AGENDA

The specific objectives and outputs of the workshop were to:

1) Conceptualize future enterprises, activities and technologies enabling the innovative capabilities and extreme performance of combinations of humans and organizations;

2) Identify human relational concepts (ReCons) that would enable these functions; and

3) Identify highest leverage ReCons and what might enable them.

An outline of the workshop agenda is shown in Table 1.

Once the Horizon is given, the HMM process generates a multitude of ideas in the general hierarchy of Table 1 and the HMM steps. Because many of the ideas do not fit traditional categories (nor do we want them to), it is necessary to collect them in novel, often metaphoric, categories. Toward the end of the workshop process the highest leverage ideas must

Introduction

Purpose, objectives and Horizon Mission Methodology background and workshop process

Leap Out of Flashlight Beam/Create New Frame of Reference (HMM Step 1-2)

❖ Provide the Horizon frame of reference
  - Describe the Horizon and the postulated world context in 2050
  - Use three themes for discussion:
  1) What could empower the African individual?
  2) What "forces" could attract humans (to contribute to an African miracle)?
  3) What institutional forces could cause dramatic change (realignments)?

Think within the New Frame of Reference (HMM Step 3)

❖ Breakout Groups - Generate alternatives characterizing this Horizon
  - What could be happening in this postulated world? Answer each theme question in terms of new inventions, enterprises, activities and human movements. Create an expansive list.
❖ Full Group - Group leaders give reports/exchange ideas
❖ Breakout Groups - Consolidate ideas and prioritize answers
  - Generate Relational Concepts (ReCons) that would be critical for enabling for priority answers

Identify Enabling Capabilities and Relationships (HMM Step 4)

❖ Full Group - Group leaders present preliminary ReCons list; exchange ideas
❖ Breakout Groups - Discussion of topics
  - Identify critical, high leverage ReCons and form novel groupings
  - For these ReCons, identify properties, implications, seeds and signals

Return to Present Frame of Reference (HMM Step 5)

❖ Full group - Reports; Display full range of ReCons
  - Collect and categorize ReCons into new functions, capabilities and metaphors
  - Consolidate concepts. Form novel groups of ReCons into new, metaphoric, integrative enterprises, capabilities and cultures
  - Identify new ecclesial roles, functions and relationships
  - If time permits, determine near-term steps and issues for high leverage ReCons

Table 1. Workshop agenda.

be selected and then near-term steps and issues identified for them. After the workshop a distillation and harvesting process must take place to further collect, organize and analyze the significance of the key ideas (ReCons) that have been generated.

Principal Results and Conclusions

The HMM workshop generated high-leverage human relational concepts (ReCons) that could dramatically change Africa. These can be arranged in many ways. (One of the areas of work using the HMM is the analysis and interpretation beginning with the harvesting and consolidation of the diverse ideas.) For this workshop two levels were selected for the organization of the resulting ReCons.

At the higher level are ReCons that are described by the HMM as higher-order approaches or higher-level insights, and may be considered as effects of the African emergence. These effects are what is "seen" outside the borders or the body of Africa: How will the rest of the world know of the African emergence? While HMM Step 5 explicitly tries to identify some of these, they occur throughout the workshop and must be harvested. Only in retrospect can we begin to understand something of their significance and interrelationships.

1) African church reformation
- ❖ Generate a world-class theology
- ❖ Broaden the *harambee* spirit

2) Africa, a source of global solutions
- ❖ Achieve ecological harmony
- ❖ Acquire unique medical knowledge
- ❖ Create African-unique economic enterprise system
- ❖ Convert integral spirit of Africa into an operational value
- ❖ Learn to treat crisis as an asset or resource

3) Twenty-first century identity
- ❖ Educate
- ❖ Use and enlarge strengths

❖ Create African movements

❖ Inspire and motivate Africans

4) Investment opportunity

    ❖ Establish stable governance and security

    ❖ Establish economic system components

      • Enterprise incubators

      • Commerce

      • Investment sources

    ❖ Feed the people

    ❖ Deliver health care

    ❖ Provide housing

    ❖ Establish transportation system

    ❖ Enable communications

Stated another way, these effects are the visions of Africa's new place in the world. Thus these ReCons can become the seeds of visions that would power the great movements of emergence in Africa.

At the lower level are high-leverage technology directions, or enabling capacities, which are the specific ReCons we set out to generate. These critical ReCons are the underlying capabilities and relationships that would power the African emergence. These are the skeleton inside the body that enables the outside effects. These critical Recons have been grouped under the appropriate visions above.

The African Phoenix is a good overall metaphor. The world stands in amazement at what has arisen from the ashes of a half century ago. This feat inspires great visions of a twenty-first century civilization rising to prominence. Stories and legends of the emergence will dominate African storytelling for many generations.

1) African Church reformation

This reformation would benefit the world for several reasons. One, a strikingly effective transformation of the traditional church will have taken place. Two, a new manifestation of the church's mission has resulted in an unprecedented level of effectiveness. Three, it is a modern church/secular miracle on a continental scale.

Generate a world-class theology

- ❖ Constitutional affirmation of human rights and religious freedom: women, children, cross-tribal
- ❖ Human solidarity in spite of religious and tribal differences
- ❖ Development of African Christian leaders who would spread a kingdom ethic across the continent, with special emphasis on outreach to government leaders
- ❖ Church functions and capabilities enabled
  - Church structures that can nurture and sustain
  - Mapping of village community life to church community
  - Increased incorporation of African forms of worship
  - Extension of African refusal to separate sacred and profane
  - Mirror African strengths in church functions
  - Creating conversations and dialogue between African independent churches and older European churches
  - Church-based Peace Corps
- ❖ Mechanisms for identifying leaders
  - African youth congress or youth ambassadors
  - Recruit transnational Christian corporate leaders
  - Horizontal church (a flat network of diverse churches)

Broaden the harambee *spirit*

Harambee is the spirit of "Let's get together and push (or pull); if all are not well, I am not well."

- ❖ Africa, the continental village. *Harambee* plus *bega kwa bega* ("shoulder to shoulder")
- ❖ Extend from village across all tribes and faiths throughout the continent
- ❖ Permeate transnational corporations, first in Africa, then globally

2) Africa, a source of global solutions

This is a great reversal of the current paradigm of Africa being only in need of such solutions. The emergence would undoubtedly be based on the strengths of Africa. A key question is how to capitalize and perhaps even institutionalize these strengths.

Achieve ecological harmony

What does this mean? Certainly not nature in its rawest form, on the one hand, nor plunder for profit on the other. Do we want harmony that is uncivilized (with disease rampant) or medically civilized (where people are healthy and fed) or economically civilized (where industry and business provide people with livelihoods)? If we want to improve the human condition, we have to disturb the universe to accommodate it.

❖ Among humans, nature and enterprise

❖ Redefinition of power (from past interpretations of "have dominion over")

Acquire unique medical knowledge

Med-Earth Corporation: medical research and pharmaceutical giants collaborate to extract the knowledge of medicines and cures latent in the genetic pool and biological diversity for illnesses now and in the future

❖ Virus/anti-virus research

Create African-unique economic enterprise system

❖ Built on *harambee*-based extended family concepts

❖ African economy and its form of free enterprise is based on *harambee*

Convert integral spirit of Africa into an operational value

❖ Africa provides model for government/economic/environmental cooperation

❖ African global network (outmigration creates overseas African network)

❖ Proactively recruit transnational executives to struggle with the issues

❖ Advocacy roles of church

❖ Wisdom of elders; preservation of heritage in facing progress

❖ Institutional embodiment

❖ Unity that honors diversity
❖ How to integrate specifics into large integrative modes
  • Specifics = problems, issues and solutions
  • New forms of analysis based on preserving the integral spirit
❖ Who would write the equivalent of the U.S. Constitution for the African integrative spirit?

Learn to treat crises as assets or resources

Adopt a different attitude about crises. Learn how to use crises positively and effectively. Africa will face many crises in the intervening decades. Why not learn to treat them as resources (maybe an unwanted resource, but not as a plague)?

3) Twenty-first century identity

An emergent Africa of 2050 would have developed a magnificent identity. It would possess a strong modern identity as well as the ancient one.

Educate

❖ Twenty-first century technology: virtual classrooms; pan-African university system with distance learning capabilities; satellite linkage for African cultural festivals.
  • African uniqueness and strengths
  • Technology for storying, orally oriented
  • Continuity of generational wisdom
  • Development of new learning methods
  • Development of new curricula
❖ Modeling/mentoring/creating new heroes
  • Future pioneers of Africa (Sesame Street version of HMM training models)
  • Network of development: not sectarian and competitive, but collaborative
  • Writing of epic poetry
  • African American sports superstars provide real and virtual clinics

❖ Popularization of communication
  • Creation of a cadre of communicators who travel across the continent
  • TV talk shows; hosts are networked together to help individual
  • Participants provide cross-fertilization of ideas (Oprah)
  • Modeling successful ventures; spotlighting examples of success

Use and enlarge strengths
  ❖ Moral voice of Africa
  ❖ Sense of purpose
  ❖ Common vision of the good; create an African ideal
  ❖ Develop methods of establishing sense of personal identity
  ❖ Edify heritage (the ancient in the midst of the modern)
  ❖ Develop the African integrative spirit into a tool of modern civilization

Create African movements
  ❖ Finding and developing charismatic leaders
  ❖ Careful selection of purposes
  ❖ Link with international movements

Inspire and motivate Africans
Encourage African expatriates and descendants, including American sports and entertainment figures, to invest financially in their ancestral continent.
  ❖ Start recovery from hopelessness with small successes
  ❖ Generate hope to liberate energy
  ❖ Identify celebratory events
  ❖ Teach Swahili as a primary continental language, English as a second language
  ❖ Incarnate the Horizons (HMM) into Africa
  ❖ Memory of past victories
  ❖ Reappraisal of past (with view to confession)

❖ Emergence of new African voices and leaders
❖ Create African movie production company to create or capture the successes and the heroic stories

4) Investment opportunity

"Unifying infrastructure" was the original category title of these items. But this bureaucratic label provides neither excitement nor promotes creative solutions. From the perspective of the rest of the world, investment opportunity is the vision that would draw the monumental capital required to develop an infrastructure of such scale.

Establish stable governance and security

Secure the continent. Without this, there is no hope within or outside Africa; no one will invest.

Establish economic system components

In the words of Frederick Douglass in 1850, "Without the means of living, life is a curse, and leaves us at the mercy of the oppressor . . ." Build relationships between Christian leaders worldwide and officials in transnational corporations, especially Christian executives, who would be encouraged to provide industrial capital for African development

❖ Enterprise Incubators
  • Cottage industries; micro loans (in Bangladesh, Grameen Bank successes) particularly for women
  • Role models and mentors, including family
❖ Commerce
  • Common currency
  • Geo-economic centers for continent
  • Pan-African passport and African common market
❖ Investment sources
  • Tourism: Africans are themselves a major market in their own continent
  • Foreign government "Marshall Plans," World Bank, charitable and mission enterprises, superstar sports and entertainment enterprises

Feed the people

❖ Food production, delivery and security

Deliver health care

❖ Safe drinking water; local medical practice

❖ Medical "Cropdusters" for vector eradication, immunization

❖ Eradication of AIDS: annual celebration

Provide housing

❖ Create the technology for the conversion of the vast resource of desert sand into habitat modules.

Establish transportation system

❖ "Afri-bahn" road system (coordinated across the continent).

Enable communications

❖ Personal cellular phones that are translator-communicators, with computer chips that automatically translate between any two African dialects.

Model of Age-Level Ongoing Organizations

Organization	Age	Resource	Approaches
Women on Mission	Adult (18 and over)	*Missions Mosaic*	Small groups choosing from several options, including prayer, Bible study, personal witnessing, mission action and so on.
Adults on Mission (coed)	Adult Adult Language Groups	*The Source* *Nuestra Tarea* (Spanish) *Our Missions World* (basic English, Korean, Chinese	
Acteens	Grades 7-12 (girls)	*Accent*	Member-led, weekly format includes Bible study, world issues, book studies, spiritual growth. Includes individual achievement plan.
Girls in Action	Grades 1-6	*Discovery and GA World*	Younger group has small group learning activities and large group sharing time. Older group participates in problem-solving and critical thinking.
Children in Action	Grades 1-6 (coed)	*Missions Matchfile*	Quarterly gatherings which include games, stories, activities from missions.
Mission Friends	Birth through Kindergarten	*Start and Share*	Experiences in which the children learn of God's love for them and all peoples. (Class for parents provides for expanding mission learning into the home.)

Participants in the Original U.S. Missions System Think Tank

Ray Bakke
International Urban Associates

Susan Doyle
Woman's Missionary Union, Southern Baptist Convention

Gary Fenton
Dawson Memorial Baptist Church

Timothy George
Beeson Divinity School/Samford University

David Hicks
Operation Mobilization

Jimmy K. Maroney
International Mission Board, Southern Baptist Convention

Grant McClung
Church of God World Mission

Paul McKaughan
Evangelical Fellowship of Mission Agencies

Betty Merrell
Woman's Missionary Union, Southern Baptist Convention

Joyce Mitchell
Woman's Missionary Union, Southern Baptist Convention

Michael Murphey
Woman's Missionary Union, Southern Baptist Convention

Dellanna O'Brien
Woman's Missionary Union, Southern Baptist Convention

William R. O'Brien
Beeson Divinity School, Samford University

Brad Ray
Oil Industry

Tom Sine
World Concern

Mike Stachura
Operation Mobilization

Bill Waldrop
Advancing Churches in Missions Commitment

June Whitlow
Woman's Missionary Union, Southern Baptist Convention

Appendix E

Taskforce: 21st Century Missions Consultation Participants*

Miriam Adeney
Regent College and Seattle Pacific University

Gerald H. Anderson
Overseas Ministries Study Center

Joyce M. Bowers
Evangelical Lutheran Church in America

Lu Dunbar
Mission Aviation Fellowship

Carol Eich
World-Christian Mobilization, Inc.

John Kyle
Evangelical Fellowship of Mission Agencies

John E. Mariner
World Witness

Jimmy K. Maroney
International Missions Board, Southern Baptist Convention

Cindy McClain
Woman's Missionary Union

Grant McClung
Church of God World Mission

Paul McKaughan
Evangelical Fellowship of Mission Agencies

Charles Van Engen
Fuller Theological Seminary, School of World Mission

Darrell Whiteman
Asbury Theological Seminary

Thomas A. Wolf
Golden Gate Seminary

Gary Fenton
Dawson Memorial Baptist Church

Kathy Giske
Presbyterian Frontier Fellowship

Steve Hawthorne
Waymakers

Paul G. Hiebert
Trinity Evangelical Divinity School

John A. Kenyon
World Vision International/MARC

Ken Mulholland
Columbia Biblical Seminary & Graduate School

Ted Noble
Greater Europe Mission

William R. O'Brien
Beeson Divinity School, Samford University

Dellanna O'Brien
Woman's Missionary Union

Bobbie Patterson
Woman's Missionary Union

Paul Pierson
Fuller Theological Seminary, School of World Mission

Larry Ragan
CultureLink

Mike Stachura
Advancing Churches in Missions Commitment

*(Wrap-up exercise for research project)

Appendix F

Mission Shift:
An Alternative Scenario

Scenario-building can be a valuable tool for dealing with the realities of the moment, and the potential for alternatives. Some planners outline patterns of preferable, possible and probable scenarios.

In the wrap-up consultation of the Taskforce: 21st Century Mission research project, one of the breakout groups modeled the kind of thinking that builds on the insights of trends, realities and future directions. This chart reflects the outcome of one group's work in articulating a preferred model for future mission endeavor.

FROM	TO
Pipeline: Unequal information access	Weblink: Equal information access
One-way street	Two-way street
Agency-based missions	Church-based missions
Churches supply the agency	Agency serves the churches
Manufactured product: missionary	Value-added service: mission
Churches support agency with individuals	Churches support individuals in agency
Should: Hierarchy employer/banker	Could: Networking broker/bridgebuilder
Missions promotion agency	Missions education of church
Long-term national missionary	Short-term international mission
Receiving missionary personnel	Receiving mission partners

MARC

Bringing you key resources on the world mission of the church

MARC books and other publications support the work of MARC (Mission Advanced Research and Communications Center), which is to inspire vision and empower Christian mission among those who extend the whole gospel to the whole world.

Recent MARC titles:

▶ *Symbol and Ceremony: Making Disciples Across Cultures*, by A.H. Mathias Zahniser. Shows how the rites, symbols and ceremonies of many cultures can be given a Christian meaning and used for discipleship. Ideal for Western Christians seeking to avoid syncretism while discipling Christians from other cultures.   183 pp. $11.95

▶ *Beyond Duty: A Passion for Christ, a Heart for Mission*, by Tim Dearborn. Designed for group or individual study, this guide restores the joy to mission by showing that it is not a duty, but a privilege that flows from our personal relationship with the God of mission.

Study guide   88 pp. . . . . $ 8.95
Leader's guide . . . . $ 2.95
Video $15.95
Complete set $19.95

▶ *Mission Handbook 1998-2000*, John A. Siewert and Edna G. Valdez, editors. Brings you key information about mission agencies in North America. Listings include all contact information to help you network effectively. Contains new research and analyses of emerging mission trends and addresses today's paramount mission concerns.
528 pp. $49.95

▶ *Street Children: A Guide to Effective Ministry*, by Phyllis Kilbourn. Equips Christians for service to children who are struggling to survive on the streets. Explains who street children are, where they can be found, why they are on the streets and the nature and extent of their trauma.   264 pp. $23.95

▶ *The New Context of World Mission*, by Bryant L. Myers. A thorough yet concise visual portrayal of the entire sweep of Christian mission. Full-color graphics and up-to-date statistics show the history of mission and reveal its future challenges.

Book .... 60 pp. $ 8.95
Slides .... 49 pp. $149.95
Overheads .... 49 pp. $149.95
Presentation Set *(one book, slides, overheads)* $249.00

▶ *With an Eye on the Future: Development and Mission in the 21st Century*, Duane Elmer and Lois McKinney, editors. Cutting-edge thinkers present essays in the fields of mission, development, education and church leadership that propose new strategies in the areas that will be vital to mission in the next century.   272 pp. $24.95

▶ *Ministry in Islamic Contexts*, Lausanne Committee for World Evangelization and the International Institute for the Study of Islam and Christianity. Concisely sets the scene for accomplishing effective Christian ministry in Islamic contexts. Summarizes recent consultation reports on this important topic.   96 pp. $6.50

▶ *Serving With the Poor in Latin America: Cases in Holistic Ministry*, Tetsunao Yamamori, Bryant L. Myers, C. René Padilla and Greg Rake, editors. Real cases and analysis of Christian ministry are presented from throughout Latin America that broaden our understanding of holism in action.   240 pp. $12.95

Contact us toll free in the U.S.: 1-800-777-7752
Direct: (626) 301-7720

 MARC   A division of World Vision
800 W. Chestnut Ave. • Monrovia, CA • 91016-3198 • USA

Ask for the MARC Newsletter and complete publications list